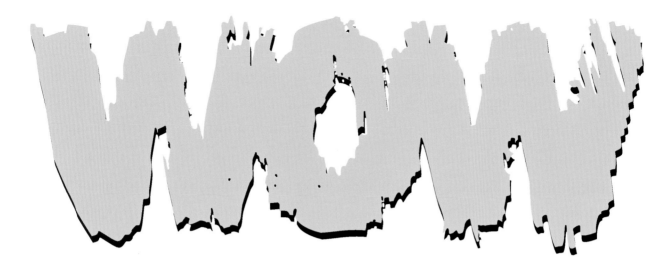

BEST OF
WWF
WCW
ECW

WORLD OF
WRESTLING

TRIUMPH
BOOKS
CHICAGO

Printed in the United States of America

This book is available in quantity at special discounts for your group or organization. For more information, contact:

TRIUMPH BOOKS
601 South LaSalle Street
Suite 500
Chicago, Illinois 60605
(312) 939-3330
Fax (312) 663-3557

Cover design by Eileen Wagner

ISBN 1-57243-351-5

contents

WWF

Exposed . . . WWF

Features

Bombshells

ECW

by Blake Norton

'Smart'
is as 'smart' does

The entire wrestling industry has waited a long, long time for a "smart" book, one which deals with the sport for what it is. Yes, wrestling is generally pre-determined. Does that mean we enjoy it any less? Not in the slightest!

The difference between wrestling and boxing, football, basketball or any other sport for that matter is that wrestling promoters discovered a long, long time ago that people don't watch sports simply for "competition," but for entertainment as well. The fact that it's mainly the competitive nature of the sport from which they derive that entertainment is merely coincidental. There are many other factors which can be just as effective in capturing one's imagination.

Wrestling has always, and will always, keep changing the mix of what it provides in its sports entertainment programs to try and match the mood of the viewers – and hopefully attract more. Some would argue that in the current climate of wrestling promotion, through the barrage of screwjobs and far-out angles, the original "competitive" nature on which the sport is based has been co-opted; but that's an argument for another day.

So what if you don't always find a contest that strictly meets the guidelines of what "competition" is? You also won't find off-seasons, walk-outs over billion-dollar contracts or pay-per-views with a 90-second main event. There's a little word known as "respect;" it takes an awful lot of respect to put a man over, to make your opponent look good for the sake of the business, and that's the only difference between our sport and any other out there.

Perhaps wrestlers don't compete (or shouldn't, at least) to score more points or try to knock one another out – but they do compete just as passionately to put on the best performance, pull off the greatest moves and get the best crowd reaction.

Personally, I'd consider the motivation behind the latter endeavors to be at least as noble as its time-tested predecessors.

Are we proud of Shawn Michaels, of Shane Douglas, Ric Flair and Steve Austin? Are we proud to be fans of the sport, and admit to what it really is, the greatest combination of competition, athleticism, raw hard work and showmanship on the planet? Are we proud that boxers, football player, and everybody else are now actually jumping on the bandwagon we created, laying out their interviews like wrestling, using entrance music like wrestling, showboating like wrestling, promoting like wrestling? Does

everyone want to be a part of the greatest show on earth?

As one prominent industry figure would say, "Oh Hell Yeah!"

Let me quickly introduce myself. My name is Blake Norton, editor of "The Bagpipe Report" (TBR) online wrestling newsletter (www.bagpipe-report.com). As many fans already know, there are numerous reports available from the so-called "sheets" – newsletters such as "The Observer," "The Torch," "The Figure Four," and many online publications including "TBR" (the largest!), "HWG" and others.

These reports bring a behind-the-scenes alternative to the so-called "mark mags," ("wrestling is real") a term which covers just about every wrestling magazine currently available in the U.S. Does that make the "smarts" better? Not necessarily, and here's why.

Because, smart is as smart does.

The strongest image which always comes to mind when I think of "the sheets" is that of Jim Duggan giving his retirement speech on "Thursday Thunder" shortly before he was

to go under the knife to try and avert his bout with cancer.

In his teary-eyed address, at one point he referred to the sheets making fun of him because of his low "workrate" and (self-imposed?) limited wrestling repertoire. At that moment, the thought that came to mind was this: "Here's a guy who started his career before any of us 'smart' guys were even around; a guy who has entertained fans for two decades; a guy who I've always respected and loved to see proudly walk the aisle with his American flag; and a guy who always had a smile for the kids and a warm attitude toward everyone I've known who've met him. And yet, he feels it necessary to refer to the callous criticism the 'sheets' have layed upon him."

It wasn't a feeling of regret on my part. "TBR" already knew he was announcing his retirement, and we gave our very best wishes, congratulating him on what had to be in anyone's book a phenomenal career. But I went surfing on the Internet that night, and the majority of references to Duggan's retirement were laden with celebratory cheer. I could-

n't, frankly, believe it! These "whiz-kids" were jumping up and down about a man having cancer! Why? Because of his supposed low "work rate."

Well, there's nothing "smart" about that at all.

But it did bring home, perhaps more profoundly than I would have liked, the fact that there are some aspects of the so-called "smart" publications I wish to be associated with ... and some that I do not.

We write about the sport of pro wrestling because we love the sport. You, the fans, want to know what's really happening in the sport because you love the sport as well. We don't aim to "expose" anyone. We don't wish to criticize unnecessarily, or cause problems for anyone. We're just here to make our contribution.

So, on behalf of the staff of "The Bagpipe Report" and everyone else contributing to WOW, I invite you to form your own opinions.

Scott Hall

Fed: WCW
Age: 40
Physical: 6'6", 288 lbs
Style(s): Brawler/Technical
Highest Accolade: WWF
Intercontinental Champion

Kevin Nash

Fed: WCW
Age: 39
Physical: 6'10", 341 lbs
Style(s): Brawler/Power Moves
Highest Accolade: WWF/WCW
World Champion

Bam Bam Bigelow

Fed: WCW
Age: 37
Physical: 6'3", 360 lbs
Style(s): Brawler
Highest Accolade: ECW World
Heavyweight Champion

Randy Savage

Fed: WCW
Age: 46
Physical: 6'3", 251 lbs
Style(s): Technical/Brawler/High-Flyer
Highest Accolade: WWF/WCW Double Champion

Lex Luger

Fed: WCW
Age: 40
Physical: 6'5", 260 lbs
Style(s): Brawler/Power Moves
Highest Accolade: WCW World Champion

rey
mysterio jr.

Sting

Fed: WCW
Age: 40
Physical: 6'2", 255 lbs
Style(s): Technical/High Flyer
Highest Accolade: WCW World
Champion

Scott Steiner

Fed: WCW
Age: 36
Physical: 6'1", 250 lbs
Style(s): Power/Technical/Brawler
Highest Accolade: WWF/WCW Tag Team Champion (with Rick Steiner)

the giant

Headed to the WWF?

bret hart
The Excellence of Execution

13

Raven

Raven Rules WCW Hardcore!

Buff Bagwell

Fed: WCW
Age: 29
Physical: 6'1", 247 lbs
Style(s): Mat Wrestler
Highest Accolade: 3-time Tag Team Champion

Buff is the Stuff!

Burn Baby Burn...

Disco Inferno

Fed: WCW
Age: 31
Physical: 6'1", 240 lbs
Style(s): Mat Wrestler
Highest Accolade: WCW TV Title

Scott Riggs

Fed: WCW
Age: 30
Physical: 6'0", 249 lbs
Style(s): Mat Wrestler
Highest Accolade: WCW Tag
Team Champion

Pretty Boy Riggs

Saturn

Fed: WCW
Physical: 5'10", 234 lbs
Style(s): Mat Wrestler brawler
Highest Accolade: WCW TV Title

Intergalactic Hardcore!

Chris Benoit

Age: 31
Fed: WCW
Height: 5'10"
Weight: 222 lbs
Style: Technical/Impact/High Flyer
Highest Accolade: ECW Tag Champ with Dean Malenko (also won WCW TV title twice against Booker T. in '98, but the WCW acknowledged neither reign.
Native Country: Canada (Edmonton)

1985

Trained in "The Dungeon," Stu Hart's legendary training room in Calgary. Others to have done so include Chris Jericho, Bret and Owen Hart and Ken Shamrock. He idolized the Dynamite Kid as a young boy and would watch tapes of him wrestling for hours on end. Benoit debuted in 1985, and would win two tag-team championships in "Stampede" wrestling before moving on to Japan.

1990

After "Stampede" wrestling folded in '89, Benoit returned to Japan to compete in NJPW, where he was known as Pegasus Kid and wrestled under a mask. Here, he perfected his high-flying and submission styles, as can be seen in his wrestling today. Pegasus defeated Jushin "Thunder" Lyger, a Japanese legend, in August for the IWGP junior title.

1991

Went to Mexico, won the WWF light-weight title (that version has long since gone unacknowledged by the WWF, not the modern-day version as worn by Taka Michinoku). He later returned to Japan.

1993

Signed a one-year contract with WCW, but was unsuccessful both in singles and as a tag team with Bobby Eaton. He returned to Japan that summer to win the "Top of the Super Junior" tournament, defeating El Samurai in the finals.

1994

Won Super J cup, beating Great Sasuke in the final. Benoit joined ECW, where he earned the moniker "The Crippler" after injuring Sabu, and later Rocco Rock.

1995

Joined forces with Dean Malenko to defeat Sabu and Taz for the ECW tag-team championships in February. Their reign lasted six weeks. Competed in a non-televised tryout with the WWF, but wasn't signed. Shortly thereafter, he joined with Ric Flair, Arn Anderson and Brian Pillman in a new incarnation of the Four Horsemen in WCW. Malenko and Guerrero also headed to WCW.

1996

Feuded with Kevin Sullivan, taking up the slack on a feud that Sullivan had with fellow Horseman Brian Pillman, who had left the federation unexpectedly. With Sullivan's real-life wife, Woman, leaving him for Chris Benoit on camera, the feud raged to epic proportions. The feud finally came to a head at the 1997 "Bash at the Beach," with Benoit defeating his arch nemesis in a retirement match.

1998

Now solo, Benoit entered several high-profile feuds in '98. He and Raven became embroiled in a major feud, which saw Benoit defeat him by submission at "Souled Out." Benoit feuded with Diamond Dallas Page over the U.S. title, wrestling an epic match at "Slamboree," despite failing to capture the coveted championship. He and Booker T. then embarked on what was considered by many as the wrestling feud of the year and met countless times in epic battles. Benoit beat Booker for two one-day reigns starting May 30. Neither reign was recognized on TV. Benoit and T. contested a "Best of Seven" series on TV (which Booker ultimately won) to decide who would face new TV champ Fit Finlay at "Bash at the Beach." Booker won back the title and Benoit defeated Finlay by pinfall the next night on "Nitro."

After several months on the shelf with an elbow injury, Benoit returned to be part of the newly reunited Four Horsemen in the fall, and is now wrestling alongside Malenko, Steve McMichael, Flair and Anderson in a bitter feud against the nWo.

WE WANT FLAIR HORSEMEN 4-LIFE

Wrestling's king of kings, Hulk Hogan, has become a legend with a 20-year-plus reign of dominance. But even the self-proclaimed **"God of wrestling"** has had to resurrect himself a couple of times over his career.

Today, the Hulk Hogan who invades our TV screens is a rippling reprobate. Clad chiefly in sinister black, he barks out his agenda of destruction to crowds all over the country. Hulk Hogan is wrestling's Darth Vader, a diabolical villain who uses his power to create chaos.

It's a far cry from times when Hogan stood for morality and truth. If the two personalities were to stand face to face inside a ring today, they would appear as different as day and night. But behind either version stands Terry Bollea, the man who breathes life into Hulk Hogan. As easy as it seems for Hogan to exist in the wrestling business, Bollea has had to live through the ups and downs to keep up that illusion.

In 1993, after a decade in the World Wrestling Federation as its signature star, Hogan was allowed to leave the company. WWF owner Vince McMahon decided that for some of the WWF's young, up-and-coming performers to reach the top, his older stars had to go. On June 13, 1993, Hogan made his last WWF title defense at the "King Of The Ring" in Dayton, Ohio.

He signed with Ted Turner's World Championship Wrestling nearly a year later after the longest time he had spent out of the wrestling spotlight. Just as it seemed Bollea had a fresh beginning in his career, an old issue threatened to destroy it. In July 1994, he was summoned to testify in federal court during McMahon's trial for steroid possession and distribution.

Bollea testified he had used various types of steroids himself from 1976 to 1989. This information contradicted statements he had made on the *Arsenio Hall Show* in 1991. Bollea said he "trained 20 years, two hours a day" to look like he did and that "I'm not a steroid abuser and I do not use steroids." During questioning, he admitted he did not tell the whole story on the *Arsenio* program and lied about his steroid use to the press.

While McMahon was acquitted later that month, Hogan's name became included in newspaper and magazine stories of steroid abuse. Though Hogan admitted to using steroids only while still legal in the United States, the public perception left his career in question yet again.

Hogan became wildly successful in his first few months in WCW. After winning the WCW title from Ric Flair in his first

Resurrecting the Hulk

Hulk Hogan survives the ups and downs, ins and outs of pro wrestling

by THE STRAIGHTSHOOTER

Hulk Hogan is wrestling's Darth Vader

On September 4, 1995, **WCW's confidence in Hogan resulted in the inception of "WCW Monday Nitro,"** a live wrestling program to run opposite the WWF's own show, "Monday Night Raw."

match, Hogan became WCW's most bankable star. Behind the scenes, Bollea was given significant power over the direction of his character. Having been brought in by Turner to impact the wrestling world on its behalf, Bollea reaped the benefits of Hogan's success. It was understood that Hogan called his own shots in WCW.

On September 4, 1995, WCW's confidence in Hogan resulted in the inception of *WCW Monday Nitro*, a live wrestling program to run opposite the WWF's own show, *Monday Night Raw*. Unfortunately, after six months of running neck-and-neck with *Raw* in the ratings, the numbers began to reflect the WWF's pulling away from its competition.

Recognizing that Hogan's name alone wasn't enough to help WCW climb over the WWF in the ratings, WCW vice president Eric Bischoff began to use Turner's considerable resources to attract other big-name talent. WCW reached deep into its pockets to lure WWF superstars Razor Ramon and Diesel to the Turner organization. Going under their real names of Scott Hall and Kevin Nash, respectively, The Outsiders (as they were billed) operated under the concept that WWF stars were invading WCW. After a few months in the company, the two inspired a surge in *Nitro* ratings, but something was still missing.

Personality Change

Bischoff began to brainstorm about how this angle could be taken to the next level. It was then that he spoke to Bollea about radically changing Hogan's character. The idea would be for Hogan to turn heel and become the third member of The Outsiders. Bollea initially opposed tearing down all that Hogan's current character had built over the years. However, Bischoff explained that this move would refresh the Hogan character, not kill it. After much consideration, Bollea agreed to take a chance.

In an event considered one of pro wrestling's defining moments, Hogan became the third member of The Outsiders on July 7, 1996, at WCW's "Bash at the Beach" pay-per-view telecast. He emerged from the backstage area to attack Randy Savage, Sting and Lex Luger in a show of unity with Hall and Nash. Then, with one sentence, Hogan cemented his new role as villain by telling the fans they "can stick it!" On that night, The New World Order was born.

Almost overnight, the *Nitro* ratings skyrocketed past *Raw* and into unprecedented heights. As leader of the nWo and WCW champion, Hogan had his most visible platform for self-promotion since the zenith of his WWF tenure. With the nWo making WCW's box-office business white hot, Bollea became entrenched backstage as ruler of the roost. After Bischoff joined the nWo later in 1996, Hogan and those close to him received the bulk of the TV time and storyline angles. Hogan, though never considered a technical great on the mat, began to draw critical reviews from all over the industry.

At "Starrcade '96," Rowdy Roddy Piper—hardly in top wrestling shape himself—gave Hogan his first clean defeat in more than six years with a sleeperhold-submission victory in their non-title matchup. Critics, fans and even the WWF referred to the cage match as "Age in the Cage," calling it a poor offering for a pay-per-view main event.

Soon after, Hogan stepped away from WCW to work on projects in film and TV. While he spent time in Hollywood, WCW turned to Hall and Nash to carry the ball. Fans began to cheer the nWo, responding to the element of "cool" that Hall and Nash provided.

In July 1997, Hogan returned to WCW and announced nefarious Chicago Bulls forward Dennis Rodman had joined the nWo. Rodman's outlandish reputation appealed to WCW fans and helped Hogan regain some fame. Unfortunately, the team of Hogan and Rodman came up short in their match against Lex Luger and the Giant at "Bash at the Beach '97." The loss began Hogan's first slump as a profession-al wrestler. He lost the WCW title to Luger in August, but got it back a week later at "Road Wild." But then he lost to Roddy Piper yet again in a non-title cage match at "Halloween Havoc."

During Hogan's slump of 1997, WCW officials were spending the year building up a Sting/Hogan match for "Starrcade '97." It was believed that Sting would become the next centerpiece of the company with the planned title victory over Hogan. However, Hogan had other ideas. In a bout that ended with more confusion than crescendo, Sting defeated Hogan for the WCW title with help from new WCW arrival Bret Hart.

But once again, Bollea made sure the Hulk Hogan character would never be far from the top of the heap for long. In early 1998, Hogan recaptured the WCW title from Randy Savage, who had defeated Sting for the belt not long before. But this time the fans were neither glad nor upset that Hogan was the champion— just indifferent.

The fans' indifference to Hogan's victory was caused by another significant moment in wrestling: the feud between Stone Cold Steve Austin and McMahon in the WWF. Austin had become wrestling's No. 1 draw and successor to Hogan's role as most visible entity. The WWF was experiencing a renaissance, climbing out from under a massive winning streak by *Nitro* in the ratings to beat it on a semi-regular basis. Ratings for *Nitro* both on TV and

pay-per-view dropped noticeably—something WCW executives did not take lightly.

By this point, a rookie performer by the name of Bill Goldberg had taken WCW by storm with an inconceivable undefeated streak and the roar of the crowds in most arenas. For the second time in his illustrious career, Hogan was about to be cast aside so younger talent could take his place.

On the first "Nitro" in 1999, Hogan returned to WCW. He shocked the world by not only re-forming The Outsiders with Hall and Nash, but winning the WCW title as Nash allowed him to take his newly-won belt from him by lying down for the three-count.

Another Fall

On July 3, 1998, Goldberg upset Hogan for the WCW title during a live *Nitro* broadcast from the Georgia Dome in Atlanta. Not only had Hogan been defeated in the ring, but Bollea was losing a political war backstage with Kevin Nash. Nash represented the new group of WCW stars who wanted to crack the glass ceiling and break out in the company. After a split in the nWo that saw Nash form his own Wolfpac apart from the black and white of the nWo, Hogan's career went into a free-fall that couldn't even be stopped when WCW brought in The Ultimate Warrior to face him.

After a disastrous pay-per-view buy for Hogan/Warrior 2 at "Halloween Havoc '98," WCW could no longer deny that Hogan couldn't carry the company. Bischoff, the man who helped Bollea revive his career in WCW, became the man who had to end it by telling Hogan to go home.

As a cover for Hogan's departure, Bollea decided to create a mock candidacy for president in the year 2000. With the stunning victory by former wrestling star Jesse "The Body" Ventura in the race for Minnesota governor, Bollea became jealous that Ventura was reaching heights that he had never reached. Fueled by jealousy and pride, Hogan announced his retirement from pro wrestling to pursue presidential aspirations on Thanksgiving night on *The Tonight Show* with Jay Leno. He used this farcical gimmick to extract the last few moments of glory from the public before he faded away.

With Hogan gone from the company, WCW used many of the younger stars who had lobbied for a chance to shine. Seeking ways to expand the visibility of his company, Bischoff negotiated with NBC about a possible series of network specials. NBC, haunted by the prospect of having the NBA lockout force a cancellation of its season and leaving lots of air time to fill, held serious discussions with Bischoff.

The last time NBC had aired pro wrestling was in the late '80s, when Hogan reigned over the WWF. Knowing that Hogan was the property of WCW now, NBC insisted that any deal would include Hogan getting lots of time in front of the camera. The network still believed the name recognition of older stars like Hogan would draw a large viewing audience. While WCW had already decided those older stars could no longer help, the thought of reaching the network before the rival WWF was too attractive to pass up.

On the first *Nitro* in 1999, Hogan returned to WCW. He shocked the world by not only re-forming The Outsiders with Hall and Nash, but winning the WCW title as Nash allowed him to take his newly won belt from him by lying down for the three-count. Bollea had once again resurrected Hulk Hogan's career, with help from NBC.

Hogan is once again on top of the wrestling mountain. But he knows that for WCW to move to the next level, it must keep him in the spotlight. "Hulkmania" may not live forever, but it will live to see another day.

For the second time in his illustrious career, Hogan was about to be cast aside so younger talent could take his place.

Old Glory Waving Again for *Hacksaw*

WCW's Jim Duggan makes an inspiring comeback from cancer

By Donny Laible

On April 5, 1999, in Las Vegas, the world's gambling playground, Hacksaw Jim Duggan left the MGM Grand Garden a richer man.

It wasn't the pull of a lever or roll of the dice that brought about this euphoric sense of fulfillment. The 22-year wrestling pro's return to the ring on *World Championship Wrestling's Nitro* reflected a message of hope in whipping his toughest competition yet in a celebrated career – kidney cancer.

"It's the fourth most common cancer in men," said Dr. Patrick Dwyer, an attending oncologist at Bassett Healthcare in Cooperstown, N.Y. "Kidney cancer is quite uncommon, but becomes more common the older a person gets."

Last winter, the 46-year-old Duggan became one of the 40,000 Americans who are diagnosed with the disease annually, according to the Bassett Healthcare tumor registry. However, after making a sobering, heartfelt speech before WCW television cameras and coming out publicly with his illness and subsequent surgery, little, if any, news on the rambunctious fan favorite was divulged by the promotion.

But when the Glens Falls, N.Y., native stomped his way from the stage to the squared circle to his familiar patriotic tune, complete with "Old Glory" slung over his shoulder and the "USA" chants initiated by Hacksaw echoing throughout the Garden, all was well again. Duggan, who began his mat career in 1977 (the same year as Hulk Hogan), had returned.

Hacksaw, who resides in central Florida with his wife and two daughters, has faced career-threatening injuries before. In 1986, after seeing two tours of competition in Asia, Duggan underwent arthroscopic knee surgery to repair injuries inflicted in the ring. Also that same year, during the then mid-South based University Wrestling Federation's championship tournament, the 6-foot-3, 270-pound Duggan received a concussion and a dent in his skull as a result of having been rammed head first into a bolt on the ring post. Up to that point, Hacksaw was the top drawing card for the better part of three years with a supporting crew that included Ted DiBiase, The One Man Gang, and "Dr. Death" Steve Williams.

Coming from behind and surprising those who said he couldn't perform up to their expectations is what one of the game's top brawlers of all time thrives on. The large scar on his right side where his kidney was removed was plain to see as Duggan performed his punches, kicks and slams on Lenny Lane for 4 minutes, 28 seconds in Las Vegas with a live national audience tuned into *Monday Nitro*, the promotion's top program. As he dropped a knee for the three-count, surely politics, egos and locker room turmoil of all types had to experience a cease fire and applauded one of their own – Hacksaw.

It doesn't matter whether it was a one-shot deal or it meant employment for Duggan as a public relations mouthpiece for WCW. Jim did it. He came back. That's all that should matter in his life outside the grappling perimeter as fuel for his future.

"In most cases, a kidney is totally removed when the tumor is limited to it. And after surgery and routine post-operative care, the individual can return to a normal schedule," Dwyer said. "As for wrestling competition, a person can do it depending on whatever discomfort he may experience in a given situation."

Duggan, whose friend and fellow wrestling superstar Big John Studd passed away after a battle with Hodgkin's Disease in 1995, also at 46, has much to reflect on with great dignity should he send a fond farewell to the game's active roster and competitive sports in general.

Long before being sized up for his first pair of wrestling boots and stepping in a ring for his debut with the then-Fritz von Erich-operated promotion in Texas, Duggan had earned the athletic tag of being a jock stud. There was a legitimate, promising football career staring him right between his eyes.

An all-state offensive guard/defensive tackle at Glens Falls High School in 1972, Duggan was recruited by several of college football's top programs, including Syracuse, Ohio State and Penn State. With four years of high school varsity experience, Jim decided to attend Southern Methodist University in Dallas. Ironically, as fate would have it, Fritz von Erich, who long before striking wrestling gold played for the SMU Mustangs, was Duggan's recruiter.

His durability was solidified in the Southwestern Conference, where Duggan compiled a record of consecutive starts as an offensive guard during his four years that remains intact today. Graduating with a degree in sociology in 1977, Big Jim, as he was addressed in his pre-Hacksaw days, had his sights set on a career in football.

A painful twist for Duggan – and a loss to the National Football League – would be wrestling's gain. While in camp with the Atlanta Falcons, Big Jim sustained a knee injury that required reconstructive surgery. He would never play a down in the NFL. Released in 1978 by Atlanta, Duggan went north for a brief tenure with the Toronto Argonauts of Canada's pro league.

Coming to the realization that he needed to concentrate on life without football, he agreed to a tryout with Fritz's boys without applying much thought to the invitation given by his SMU recruiter to give wrestling a try. After making his ring debut in September 1977 as a fill-in for a tag team contest, Duggan's life would forever change.

It was in an era when high flying, suicidal moves were not only the oddity but a rarity, and individual gimmicks assigned by promoters to their talent were tame by today's standards. Big Jim Duggan would comfortably march among the wrestling soldiers who were not among the exceptional, but among the masses that try harder than the ordinary.

With Lenny Lane in Las Vegas, Duggan didn't pull any surprises. Dating back to making spot appearances on World Wide Wrestling Federation shows promoted in New York's Capital District and western Massachusetts by Ted Bailey, what you see is what you get with Duggan's performances. They're nothing fancy, but when booked properly, they're financially successful.

It was with the hard-line, old-school promoter Bill Watts that Duggan became a name, a draw in wrestling in the mid-South. Main events with Buzz Sawyer and Dick Slater added stock to his popularity and personal bargaining power. In 1986, Hacksaw Jim shifted allegiances to Vince McMahon's World Wrestling Federation, and by 1987 he became one of the company and industry's most recognizable figures over the following decade.

After many successful years with the federation, with his limited ring skills deteriorating, Duggan, mainly for the recognition factor, was brought aboard WCW.

As a cancer survivor, the comeback in Las Vegas had to inspire a liberated, cleansing feeling to the flag-toting, 2x4-carrying ring veteran. Duggan, an object at times of feverish curiosity, is a hero to his peers, wrestling fans, and all Americans in particular. No wrestling terminology can equal hearing the three most precious words Jim Duggan will hear in the near future – "Happy Father's Day" from his daughters.

Diam In the Rough

Diamond Dallas Page Goes from Zero to Hero in a Bang!

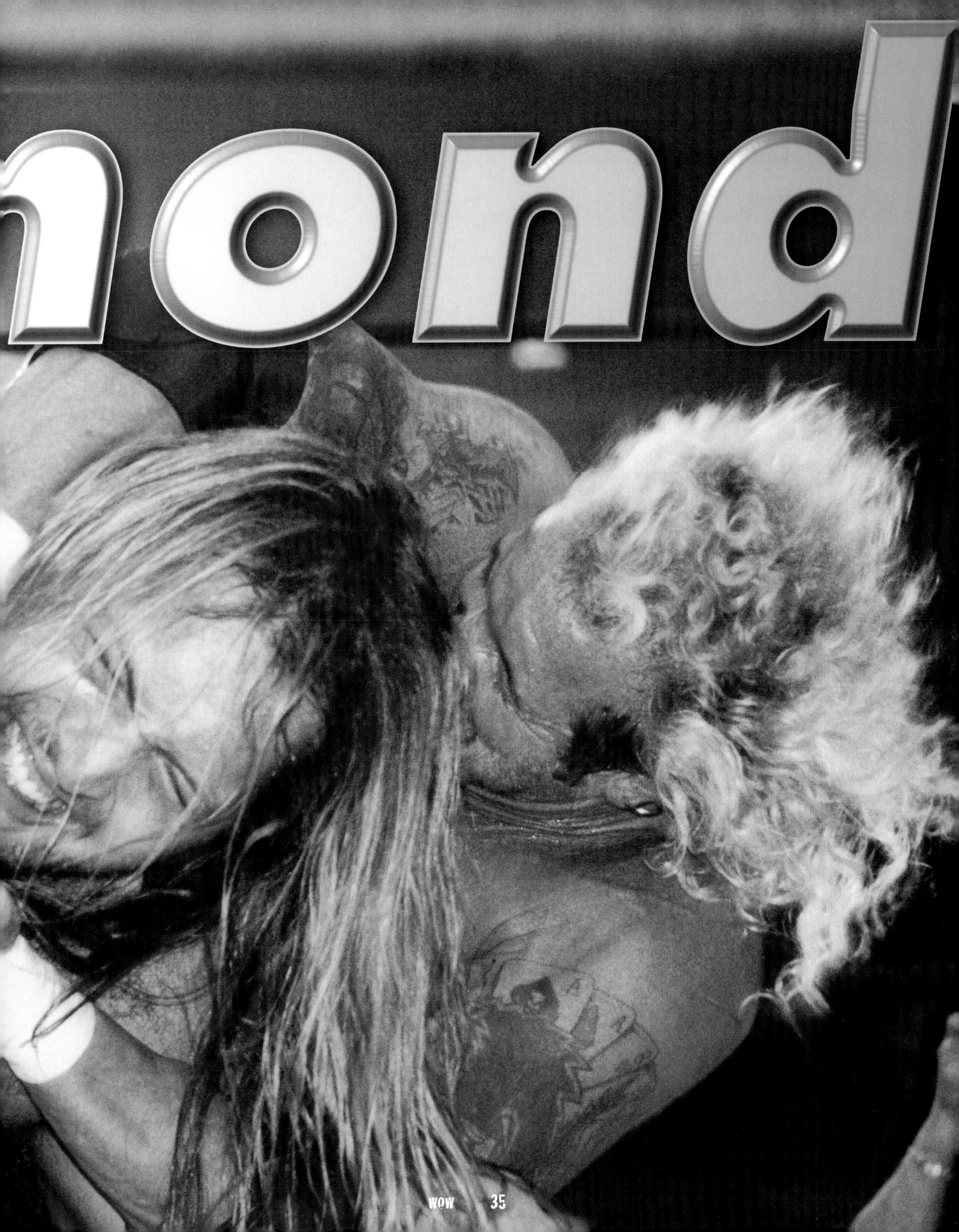
nond

Blake Norton had the chance to sit down with former U.S. Champion Diamond Dallas Page to talk about his life and times.

During the 90-minute conversation, Page was twice interrupted by the doorbell, both times concerning the charity work he does on a regular basis – attending fund raisers, contributing money and donating wrestling gear and memorabilia for auctions.

In the ring, Page has a reputation for being the most hard-working and deserving star in wrestling today, period. He constantly searches for ways to improve his repertoire and put in a better performance, as is evident from watching any of his matches. Beyond all else, Page is one of the few remaining men in the sport who is not a mark for himself. He loves to see an angle "work." He doesn't have to get the three-count; he's just as proud getting a guy over that no one else could or putting on a match that makes everyone else stand back and say "hey ... that's something."

Taking Time Off

DDP: Mainly I wanted to be down, and be off TV for a while. I thought, "I don't want (the fans) to be sick of me, I've worked too hard!" You know, that's the bottom line, when I come back, I want to definitely have more of an edge. I think I've been way too serious lately. One feud after another is just becoming too serious, and it's limiting my character. I'm watching what's working, and I just think you have to be more entertaining, sometimes funny ... 'cause I can be pretty much of a smartass, and I haven't been showing that side of me. I went to go see the movie *Payback*. It stars Mel Gibson. Mel plays a convict. Ex-con, pickpocket, thief, bank robber, murderer ... and he's the babyface.

BN: (laughs) That's the '90s for you.

DDP: That's what I'm talking about. (both laugh) That's where I'm going with that. You know there's got to be an edge all the way around, to be ... even John Wayne, who was probably the greatest babyface of all time. He had a lot of humor. I'm not gonna take myself seriously, you know, 'cause in this day and age, if you take yourself too seriously, people are gonna say "f--- that."

Work Ethic

BN: I was watching "Halloween Havoc" when you took on Goldberg. That had to be the best main event of the year. It was really something.

DDP: You know, when I look at that, I will always pick me out of anything. They say, "What about that guy, and that guy?" If there's a better match (under) 15 minutes, I want you to show it to me. I thought to myself, "If you HATE these, how could you not put that match over?" It had every element of drama, without a f----n' angle, plus it had intensity up the ass. To be perfectly honest, I didn't yell, I found Goldberg, it's a shoot. I talked him into being a wrestler for six years, and when he finally comes in a year and a half later, we hand him into the double main event. And in a match to be that good, I could never dream for him, you know? And that's a match that I lost and walked out of stronger. I lost it to Goldberg, I beat and lost to Bret Hart, I beat the Giant, then I lost to Steiner on *Nitro*. It's all just give and take. One way or the other, you know? You can survive it all, if you have a character. He gets to develop his character, and it'll come, you know? You should never be in that position, right now, he's two years away from being in that position. But he got so hot.

Where it All Started

DDP: I debuted in the AWA in 1988, probably April or May. I came in as a manager. I did that for about nine months, managing Badd Company. Then I went to Col. Beers, then Medusa. You know, I was working one day a week, we were doing four shows.

I was a nightclub guy, who could f----n' talk, and they had no idea I was 6-foot-5. They saw my tape and said, "We want to bring you and your boys in." There was one problem. There were no "guys" on the tape. I said, "I ain't got no boys." They looked at me funny. I said, "Well, I'm ready," you know? And that's how it happened. They told me to come up there, they said, "Bring Badd Company, bring some of those hot girls of yours, and we'll give you a tryout. If we like you, we'll use you ... if we don't, we

won't." I was like "Oh, OK." (laughs) I was working there, and I also worked Florida Championship Wrestling. I did color commentary with Gordon Solie, I didn't know a wristlock from a wristwatch. Gordon really helped me with a lot.

BN: He's one of the best.

DDP: Oh God, I would just feed off of him, you know? I'll never forget my tryout with the WWF for play-by-play. I got there, and it was like, "Don't do this, don't do that, don't say 'baby,' don't say 'Good Gawd.' " They were killing everything I say, you know? They had me do my play-by-play as a rib, and I smoked it. Lord Alfred Hayes looked back at me, pulled out his chair and said, "That was excellent. Where did you ever learn to do play-by-play like that?" So I sat next to Gordon Solie for two years. You learn, whether you want to or not. I could never do it today like that, but after working with him, it was like, who knows? So I managed there, I did color, then I quit the bar business. I came up here full time as a manager and commentator. Brought in Scott Hall ...

BN: When Razor Ramon essentially started ...

DDP: That's what kills me about Vince, saying that he created the Razor Ramon character. If there's a difference between Razor Ramon and the Diamond Studd, besides razor blades on the outfit, I want to know what they are. I created that gimmick, that look, everything. It's kind of too personal to tell you. Then it got to a point where, realistically,

vas a kid,

"I always liked the bad guy and the good guy. I loved Dusty Rhodes when he was a babyface, I loved him when he was a heel."

DDP, back in the day.

taught me the "Golden Cravat." So now, any TV announcer wants the guys to throw a bunch of s---. I put that Cravat on your head, I'll make you cry like a bitch. I mean, if I wanted to put you in the Diamond Cutter, you have no f----n' choice, zero, nada. You know, it's the hold that's put on. So, I added that to it, and one day at Jake's, I said, "Let's try a suplex. Guts, back, snapped ... BANG." First time I ever said "bang." He looked at me and smiled, smoking a cigarette. He says, "Man, you got it. It's the quickness of the move that makes the people pop." I looked at him and said, "You never see it coming, it's that quick." It became a line later on.

I stayed late at the Power Plant, coming up with different ways

to do the move. Other guys came up with ways for me. Independent guys would send me tapes and say, "Try this." I've always searched for other ways. Another way, people never see me coming. It's just BOOM and BANG. Other times when they think they have it and don't, I've seen sides of buildings stand up at a time. A camera shot of 4,000 people standing, at a time.

BN: Yeah, when you hit on the Giant (at "Starrcade"), that came out of nowhere. Schiavone nearly wet his pants.

DDP: My favorite one was the parking lot one, where I did it to Savage. That's where things got big for me, the time where I didn't go nWo. They now had all these players, and it was down to me and Sting. What a guy to be rubbed up against. Me and

Sting, fighting with the guys. Ultimately, they wanted me to be part of the whole deal, but I've never been a gang guy. I wanted to just hang there and do my own thing.

Turning Down the nWo

DDP: I shook Scott Hall's hand on that *Nitro*, and when I went to pull away I caught him in the Diamond Cutter. That was the second loudest pop I've ever heard. NOBODY saw it coming. Some of the people wanted me nWo, a lot of people were thinking "aw, f---, not him too!" But when I popped (Nash) too, that was the first time I ran through the crowd (Page does it regularly now), and I was the first guy to get away from the nWo, through the crowd, and people were going crazy! The Feud with Savage was definitely what made me, it was beating Savage the first time out.

BN: That's when you became a main event name, when at any given time they could say, "Let's put Page in the main event."

DDP: Exactly, on any *Nitro* or whatever. He made me, then he killed me (in the ring), and he got more heat than anybody; and I want to know who has more heat than Scott Steiner right now.

BN: Good point. When (Steiner) first went singles, nobody was into him, but with Kimberly in the middle, it's gone crazy.

DDP: Yeah, and he's going to push the envelope all the way. Certain people, these "freaks" he has out there, are going to love him. I mean, when I was a kid, I always liked the bad guy and the good guy. I loved Dusty Rhodes when he was a babyface, I loved him when he was a heel; I loved Jake Roberts when he was a face, but also when he was a heel. There are people who are going to go both ways, especially with the nWo Wolfpac, they're so strong. (Oakland) was probably THE worst place to do that match. Looking back on it, I'd never have done that match there. I'd have waited for somewhere down South, or Midwest, even Chicago. But if you weren't talking about nWo country, Oakland has to be No. 1, period! (laughs)

BN: It was very evident all night long, the strong anti-face presence.

DDP: Oh yeah man, the Black and Red was everywhere. They loved the bad guys, that's gang central! (laughs) But Savage was great for me, those feuds were great for me.

"Feel the Bang" Video

DDP: I just did the DDP *Feel The Bang* video. It has great high-

Top: DDP with Minnesota Gov. Jesse "The Mind" Ventura.
Bottom: DDP with All-Pro 49ers wide receiver Jerry Rice.

lights from all the matches with me and Savage, it has highlights all over. It's a pretty good video all the way around. It picks up around the time of the nWo; I would have loved for it to start earlier, because people love that old s---. The stuff they didn't know, especially for the new fans. But over that period, going nWo with Savage, that's what turned the corner in my career.

Diamond Cutter Man

DDP: The biggest thing I've gotten over. It was a period when they still wouldn't book me with the main event guys, I just started talking about the Diamond Cutter. I figure I'll make the diamond cutter and get that over. People still come over and say to me "Diamond Cutter man" instead of DDP.

I was pulled over with the Giant (Paul Wight) one night, we were driving like idiots. This cop was cutting a promo on me like you wouldn't believe; I was thinking I was toast. We were trying to get out of the arena. People were going crazy, we were probably driving over them and s---, we were driving a 4x4, so forget about it! (both laugh)

I tried talking about the wrestling, but he was so angry, he was blasting through me. He had to be two minutes through this promo when Giant leans over and says, "Listen sir, we're very sorry, we were just trying to leave the arena," and he backs up, looks at Giant, looks at me, looks at him, looks at me ...

He makes the diamond cutter sign, and screams "DIAMOND CUTTER MAN!" "Yeah!" "I LOVE YOU!" He'd gone in two minutes from "f---you" to "I love you." He goes "Oh my god! Giant! DDP! You guys be careful, drive safe, and watch out for these crazy people!" About a minute later, he pulls us over again, and says, "I gotta get an autograph!" So obviously the hand thing, it all worked. (both laugh)

After Savage

DDP: The biggest pop I ever heard was when I pulled off the La Parka Mask (on *Nitro*, after taking on Randy Savage in disguise). They went nuts. Then it slid right over to Hogan. We never had that singles match with any real finish, but the tags, with (basketball player Karl) Malone, other people can say what they want about it, but it would never be at fever pitch without it. (Dennis) Rodman was typical Rodman, but when Malone said, "I'll get in the ring,"... Here's not only one of the greatest basketball players of all time, which he is, he was MVP the year before and should have been last year, but he's looked up to by so many people, that when he said, "I love wrestling, I want to be in it," the rest of the world went "REALLY?" And (Jay) Leno did it too, everybody said, "What?" People say it was a comedy match but it wasn't. Leno did a phenomenal job; for who Jay Leno is. He wasn't even a baseball player (laughs), and out of the three – basketball, football, ballplayers – I'd rather go for basketball, the guys are more agile than a football or ballplayer. Basketball players do it all. John Stockton, he's one of the most difficult players in the game. Those guys getting involved took wrestling to the next level, they mainstreamed it. For me to be part of that is unbelievable. In 10 years, I'll be "the guy who wrestled with Jay Leno or Karl Malone." Then it went on to Bret Hart, trading that (U.S. title) back and forth.

BN: There was a great series of matches in there.

DDP: Yes, there was ... The Bret Hart thing put me with the Giant at the end of the year, and I don't know any other people who have actually pinned the Giant with their finisher except for me. That's something that's always going to be there.

"...all this strength, taking me, spinning me, dropping me on his knee. Usually I'd try to catch my feet to absorb some of the impact, but it didn't happen."

BN: It was a hell of a picture to see you fly through the air from the top turnbuckle onto his head, hitting the Diamond Cutter on Giant (at "Starrcade"). It's just one of those unforgettable moments, it's like a defining moment; it's just so hard to miss, because the two of you guys together are going at, like, 12 feet in the air, easily. (laughs)

DDP: Yeah. It was a total Big Man – Monster Man match. If you watch the backbreaker he gave me, which I taught him how to do, from the double-choke into the backbreaker ...

BN: That was a killer.

DDP: ... all this strength, taking me, spinning me, dropping me on his knee. Usually I'd try to catch my feet to absorb some of the impact, but it didn't happen.

BN: He's just so high ...

DDP: Yeah, I wrapped around him like a "U!" It hurt so bad. That was the bump I want to show, I'm not sure if Eric (Bischoff) will let me show the footage, but both him throwing me through the floor (on *Nitro*) and the backbreaker spot there is just brutal.

How they had a side shot of Steiner when he had me in that recliner (at "Superbrawl"), I want to strangle the director, because the front sight of Steiner pulling back, and me choking out are unreal.

BN: Yeah, the eyes were floating back in your head, and everybody was like, "Jesus, is that guy okay?"

DDP: There you go again, the element of doubt, but I was hurting like (crazy). People don't get how hard it gets out there. Never mind the guy getting the push, who deserves it. And he's a bad mother. Disco is a tough guy. He's not a fighter, but he's a tough guy, he gets the s--- beaten out of him, and people don't give the guy his respect. They don't realize; they think he's hitting a bed. NOT! I wish it was! I could do this a lot longer! (laughs) Another three years and I'm done! (laughs)

BN: I get a lot of guys asking me about the "trampoline." It's weird, you can show people a 400-pounder hitting the mat, and it barely moves. It makes no sense. It all goes back to the quote, "The people who believe ..." I think Jeff Jarrett said it, but maybe he took it from someone else ...

DDP: That was a great line.

BN: "For the people who believe, you don't need to explain, and the people who don't believe, no explanation is good enough."

DDP: That was a GREAT quote. I've said it a hundred times.

BN: Me too! (both laugh together)

"Yeah, I wrapped around him like a 'U!' It hurt so bad."

The "Smart" Fans

DDP: The guys on the Internet, I respect and like. They're the only things I'll read. I won't read anything from Keller. They made me believe they were the norm, but they're not the norm. They are so off the norm they're not on the same planet. The only "smart" audience I give a s--- about is the Internet. The Internet is growing every day, one of the reasons why we've got 15,000 members (on the Union of Diamond Cutters list). I shoot to a certain degree, but I don't go all the way, they like that element of doubt, they like that little grey area. The booking committee said I could never be a top guy. What do you mean I'll never be a top guy? "Well, you won't be!" And after three months of beating guys, to have someone come up and say, "This Page push, it's gotta stop." I said, "Oh really? Get one of those mothers, I want to talk to them now." "Oh no, we can't do that." "Well then don't tell me," I said, "because that's bulls---, I've busted my balls like nobody else ever has. If there's someone who doesn't really believe that they have to tell me to my face."

There's nobody I won't go up to and say, "This is the situation, what's the deal." I'm not afraid to do that to Meng, and he's one of the baddest men in our business. Thank God he's one of the sweetest, too.

I laugh when radio jocks who aren't marks come up to me and say, "You guys don't really get mad at each other, do you?" I say, "There's no ego in your business, is there?" That's the most ego-driven business in the world.

Sometimes it gets a little too real. It gets WAY too real. It goes back to the Jeff Jarrett quote, because you still can't make some guys understand. But as far as the big picture in general, I'll come back with the Steiner thing, I'm going to be the same guy, but I'm going to have more of an edge, and I'll be funnier. Why leave the heels (to) do all the funny s---? ... Just because of being a "good guy" I wouldn't say something before; now I'm gonna! People like to be entertained, they want to laugh.

BN: The fans like it a lot more if the stars have fun themselves. It's always been that way, Disco Inferno, the lower card you can definitely see it. People just take to them a lot more.

DDP: Without question.

The Movie "First Daughter"

DDP: I don't want to be a movie star; I want to do movies, I don't want to be like, "Sting does this thing, Hulk Hogan does that;" I just want to do a couple of movies. We have this one called *First Daughter*, where we're kidnapping the president's daughter. I'm not sure when it will be out, but I'm heading to Australia for 10 days. I'm going to take some time down here, being home, eating all the time, training. I feel so much better already. My body needed this time to go through rehab. And marquee names rise value-wise. Look at Sting – they're going to pop huge when he comes back. Rick Steiner got a huge pop coming back. I don't want to be gone too long; it will be explained in an interview. I think any artist, when you do too much, people get tired of you.

The Book

DDP: I'm so happy with it. I'll be curious to see how professional editors handle it; I can't see what they'll actually cut. I've edited it three times; we're about 10 chapters in right now. They'll clean it up verbiage wise, spacing wise, whatever, but this really gets into the stuff that the real fans who love wrestling will dig it, but they won't want to know what happened to you when you were 5. This is 1/8 of my life; it's some of the high points, and really, really low points. The front page will be a quote, "I've been into the penthouse and back to the s--thouse so many times, my life is like a yo-yo, but the sting is getting shorter." I said that line to Smokey, and I looked at him, he looked at me, and said that has to be in the book. I said, "It's going to be the first line. Definitely."

Some of the stories are just incredible. It gets into the first time I met Bischoff, a lot of shoot stuff, where a lot of guys will be saying, "Wow, you're kidding!" When people realize that he never gave me s---. He said it two years ago, that being his friend isn't an advantage. He can go the other way with nepotism; when he ultimately believed in me, it really became an advantage. Who else would go back and forth to L.A. every day to train Jay Leno? I was sleeping three or four hours a day for 24 days, I'm not kidding. I was one of the few people he knew he could put in that spot and knew I wouldn't bitch, ever, and just thank God I was in the spot.

BN: You have a reputation for that.

DDP: You just gotta take advantage. Nobody wants to hear bitching. Just take advantage of what you've got.

The music pounds. A solitary figure appears ... black boots ... black knee wraps ... black briefs ... black-padded gloves and black elbow pads — warrior accessories on a frame that has been ripped and chiseled from years of intense exercise, weight training, and dedication to excellence.

By Larry Burnett

You are standing in your underwear in front of thousands of raucous, rowdy fans. You turn around and a high-powered, bald-headed behemoth catapults into your rib cage. Your body crumbles and your lungs try not to collapse. You've been "speared" – planted in the canvas – by

GOLDBERG!

The Ironic Inside Story

You are exhausted, beaten up, barely standing.

His story is almost impossible to believe. In the late 1980s, Goldberg (yes, that is his real name) grabbed All-Southeastern Conference honors as a ruthless, predatory nose tackle at the University of Georgia. *Football News* named him second-team All-America behind Illinois' Mo Gardner, Notre Dame's Chris Zorich and USC's Tim Ryan.

Suddenly, your head is forced down, then crammed between bulging biceps, pumped-up pecs and a sweaty armpit. You feel a tug and yanks your leg for leverage. You vaguely hear a "1-2-3," a slapping sound on the mat and a bell.

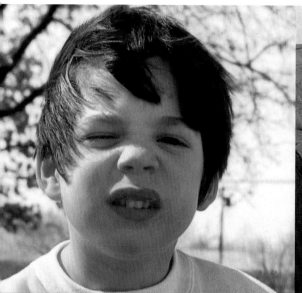  

at your waistband. Before you know it, your head is down, your feet are up, your toes are tap-dancing in the sky. This mammoth mass of muscles dangles you there, upside down, toying with you. You cannot break free!

Finally, the attack is over. The bulky body sets you free. You are flattened and can't get up. There is a deafening roar from the crowd and a maniacal, animal-like roar from the creature that just demolished you. You've

Just for perspective, a pretty good lineman from the University of Miami, Russell Maryland, was a third-team pick that year.

Goldberg earned his accolades with hard-nosed play and tenacity. His powerful head-knocking play and his aggressive hand-to-hand combat in the collegiate ranks also earned the four-year letterman a reputation. Goldberg was the featured attacker in Georgia's "Junkyard Dogs" defense. He'd chase down, rough up and bite into opponents. And when his teeth unclenched, Goldberg would bark right in their faces. His Georgia glory days were Goldberg's proving ground for attaining his life-long dream of playing in the National Football League.

You are at his mercy, suspended, blood rushing to your head, awaiting your fate ... waiting ... waiting ... and then – BLAM!

Your opponent stands tall, then pivots. Your torso does a half twist in midair. Your back leads the way as your body tumbles and starts to drop. Your weight crashes to the mat and a 285-pound monster comes along for the ride, crushes the air out of you, forces your shoulders into the canvas,

been "Jack-Hammered" and pinned by GOLDBERG!

Don't feel bad and don't bother getting up. You are just another step on the road to the top, traveled by one of the hottest shooting stars in the history of professional wrestling – Bill Goldberg!

Unknowingly, those Bulldog battles "between the hedges" may have also set the stage for Goldberg's current career in World Championship Wrestling.

Goldberg's grit and determination at Georgia got him drafted in 1990 by the L.A. Rams. He went in the 11th round, much later than he ever expected. When he finally got to play in the NFL, he didn't exactly tear up professional football, but he did manage to tear up various parts of his body on numerous occasions. In fact, his stints with the Rams and Atlanta Falcons were a blur of injuries, disappointments and frustrations.

Reality, though, was seeping in for Goldberg and was tough to face. His bank account was dwindling and his options were limited, at best.

"There really weren't any," Goldberg explained. "I could go back to school, could work as a personal trainer, which is a dead-end job, or I could get a regular job like everyone else."

"I had to try to find something that my football career could carry over to," he added. "All the years, all the blood, sweat and tears that I sacrificed to get where I was in the NFL game. I knew there had to be something out there that likened itself to pro football. It was very limited! To be able to compare something to professional athletics, it's quite hard. So, I had to search high and low. Wrestling was always an option. It was always

Finally, in 1994, major stomach surgery forced Goldberg to hang up his helmet and put his NFL dream to bed, way too early.

"Anybody who aspires to do something their entire life, then finally gets there and doesn't accomplish what they wanted to accomplish, you're gonna feel like you sold yourself short," Goldberg said in an exclusive interview.

"In a way, I did, but, hell, once I look back on it, what is the percentage of people who even make it there? So that keeps me going."

At the age of 28, Goldberg's chase for a high-profile NFL career was over.

Professional wrestling was barely in his thoughts and definitely not on his short list of "things to do" to replace the thrill, excitement and competition of NFL football.

"Throughout my entire life, I've known, and realized, that I AM NOT LIKE ANYBODY ELSE. I WANT TO BE DIFFERENT. I DON'T WANT TO FOLLOW THE SAME PATH."

an option. It was never in the back of my mind that I would actually take the option."

In fact, Goldberg was adamantly opposed to climbing into the wrestling racket at that time. During his college days at Georgia, and his NFL-playing days with the Falcons, Goldberg had rubbed shoulders in the Atlanta area with several professional wrestlers. Goldberg worked out at Main Event Fitness, the gym owned by Lex Luger and Sting, in Doraville, Ga. He impressed them with his size, strength, agility and personality, but Goldberg made it clear – he wanted nothing to do with their sport.

"They always put it in my ear, 'Well, you'd be a good wrestler. You've got the look and you're athletic.' I just said, 'You've got to be kidding! I'd never do that!' I have a lot more pride in myself than to go out there in

my underwear and wrestle in front of millions of people."

Then Goldberg laughed and said, "Look at me now! When I made that statement, it was prior to me finding out how much money these goons make."

MY, HOW TIMES CHANGE

Fast forward to now.

This football guy who never wanted to be a professional wrestler is now in his second season with World Championship Wrestling. He has taken the sport by storm. Goldberg brings a "no-nonsense, take-no-prisoners" approach to the craft. His incredible crowd appeal and marketability have rocketed the former nightclub bouncer on the fastest track ever to wrestling superstardom.

Goldberg's goateed mug is a fixture on the covers of just about every wrestling magazine, and he has made his mark in the mainstream as well with a cover for *TV Guide, People, The New Yorker, Rolling Stone,* and *Spin. The New York Daily News* and *USA Today* jumped on his story and so did *EXTRA*, the tabloid TV show. Last fall, Goldberg made his acting debut on *Love Boat: The Next Wave*, and the 32-year-old wrestler will be seen in the fall of '99 on the big screen starring opposite Jean Claude Van Damme in *Universal Soldiers: The Sequel.*

Not bad for a reluctant wrestler. **Incredible for the WCW, which almost let Goldberg slip through its bare knuckles in 1996 — to its rival, the World Wrestling Federation.**

"I came up with a wrestling idea that I thought was different. Nobody else had done it," Goldberg recalled. "With the package I brought to the table, I thought I could be different. I thought I could be successful, with my work ethic and my martial arts background, and me training so hard. If I put my mind to it, I think I can do just about anything. So, I finally put my mind to it."

Goldberg was in great shape, muscular from years of workouts and preparation for the wars of collegiate and professional football. He was 6'4," 285 pounds and "cut." His chiseled physique was tailor-made for wrestling, and his shaved head and trademark antlers tattoo on his left shoulder didn't hurt "the look."

Goldberg figured that his football background and training, combined with his hard-nosed tenacity and desire to learn the wrestling game, would give him an innovative approach to the business – one that,

Goldberg on the set of the "Love Boat"

Goldberg hoped, would land him a shot at professional wrestling's big paydays.

"I made a call to Eric Bischoff (President of World Championship Wrestling) and I inquired," Goldberg said. "Then I went to an event with Lex and Sting. I talked with Bischoff a little bit more and inquired more. They never called me back! And then I said, 'Time is running out here!' So I contacted the WWF. They made me an offer and it was terrific and everything, but it was just so hard."

Goldberg was offered a solid, seven-year, guaranteed deal by the WWF and was just hours away from signing it when the WCW finally called. He was miffed that

Bischoff had taken such a long time to show interest in him, but Goldberg also had misgivings about hooking up with the World Wrestling Federation.

"Number one, I didn't know anybody up there (at the WWF)," Goldberg said. "Number two, I didn't want to move to Connecticut. I was in the process of trying to buy a house, so it just wasn't the right time for me to get up and move. So, finally the WCW gave me a call. The morning of my meeting with the WWF for my contract signing. They called me that morning!"

Goldberg postponed his WWF signing to hear what Bischoff had to offer, and in September of 1996, he signed a developmental deal with World Championship Wrestling. It basically came down to opportunity, familiarity and location, location,

location. The house that Goldberg was buying was located outside of Atlanta, the home base for the WCW.

"No question, that made all the difference in the world," Goldberg admitted. "That, and the fact that I knew so many of the people here. I felt like I was, kind of, at home."

But wait a minute! Wrestling? Goldberg's NFL career had been punctuated by a laundry list of injuries. How could he expect to survive, with no pads and no helmet, in the rugged world of professional wrestling? With all the travel, all the lifts, flips and flops? In 1993, when he was with the Falcons, Goldberg suffered what appeared to be a severe groin injury, but he still limped his way through the entire NFL schedule. Then, during the offseason, he had surgery to repair the painful problem. Goldberg had to have the operation. It was a necessity, but it killed any chance he had of hooking on with the brand-new Carolina Panthers, who had picked him in the 1994 expansion draft.

"I decided right after the Falcons' season," Goldberg remembered. "Team doctors are team doctors. They're self-serving in the sense that they want to get you ready, or they want to do whatever they can to make you a part of the team, if you are valuable enough. I wasn't happy with their diagnosis. I found my own doctor and bing, bang, boom, he found out what the deal was. I got it operated on and got it taken care of."

"Unfortunately, it took me a long time to recover and I went to Carolina right after my surgery and I couldn't even walk. I couldn't even jog. So I was on this expansion team, but I was hurt and couldn't perform for about a month while they were trying to put a team together. It was the

worst scenario I ever could have imagined!"

Get this! Goldberg's injury wasn't just a groin pull. He had torn the stomach muscle right off his pelvic bone. Dr. William Meyers, now the chairman of surgery for the University of Massachusetts Memorial Medical Systems, reattached the abdominal muscle with an innovative procedure that he had used on the NHL's Claude Lemieux, soccer's Eric Wynalda and many others.

"People didn't understand it very well and thought if it wasn't a hernia, you shouldn't operate on the groin for this sort of thing," Dr. Meyers explained. "The main abdominal muscles insert on the pubis and the adjacent ligaments. Basically, there is a rip and they are torn away. What you do (to fix it) is create a broad band of attachment so you are reattaching and reinforcing the muscle so that it doesn't rip again."

Dr. Meyers has a 96 percent success rate with these procedures, but Goldberg's surgery happened so close to the Panthers' mini-camps that he didn't have time to recover and never got to show his true stuff. Carolina waived Goldberg. His NFL window of opportunity slammed shut in the spring of 1994.

The surgery, however, was a success.

Three years after the operation, Goldberg was a headliner for the WCW, leaving opponent after opponent in his wake and putting more strain on his abs and groin muscles than the rigors of the NFL ever did.

His signature move, the "Jack Hammer," is a vertical suplex. Goldberg lifts incredibly large wrestlers (for example, the 550-pound "Giant"), turns them upside down, holds them in the air, then pivots, rides his opponent's chest to the canvas and hammers him into the mat for the pin.

Holy abdominals, Goldberg! Even your surgeon can't believe what you're up to.

"Our aim is to get athletes back to pre-

vious performance status, or above," Dr. Meyers explained. "I've achieved that, fortunately, in most of the patients that I have operated on. But I still can't imagine doing the sort of stuff he (Goldberg) is doing. That's impressive to me, no matter who it is! Absolutely! It's very impressive!"

Goldberg learned the wrestling "ropes" during three months of intense training and workouts at the WCW's Power Plant training site in Atlanta.

Plant director Dwayne Bruce pushed Goldberg through concentrated, one-on-one sessions to get him ready for the ring. Those sessions led to practice (dark) matches in Orlando. With the help of Bruce, Goldberg caught on quickly and found that there wasn't much he couldn't do.

"(Bruce) is the leader of the Power Plant, and if it wasn't for him, I wouldn't be where I am now." said Goldberg, his voice tensing as he continued. "Bischoff just thought I was another football player who wanted to wrestle. Dallas Page has helped me along the way, but in no way, shape, or form has any one person molded me, molded my career more so than Dwayne Bruce. Anyone out there who takes credit for it (and Dwayne wouldn't take credit for it) is full of it."

At The Plant, Goldberg soaked up all the wrestling technique and "know-how" he could handle. It was there that he answered any, and all, questions about his strength and durability by learning and mastering the "Jack

Hammer."

"I picked up that big giant guy, Reese (who is close to 500 pounds)," Goldberg said. "He was the guy I originally formed the move on. I figured if I could do it to him down at the school, I could do it to anybody. You always worry about past injuries. Unfortunately, when people focus on that, they always get hurt! The thing I do is: I don't even think about it. I feel that if I'm prepared enough, physically, to go in there, then I'm prepared enough to do whatever it takes to perform."

THE DEBUT

Goldberg got his first chance to perform – on live national television – on Sept. 22, 1997, in Salt Lake City, Utah. It was *WCW Monday Nitro* on TNT. He was still called "Bill Goldberg" back then. There was no special introduction, no fanfare, no exciting entrance. Truth is, that night, when WCW announcer Tony Schiavone introduced Bill Goldberg for the very first time, he played up the fact that this new guy in the ring was a virtual unknown in professional wrestling circles.

"We have a newcomer, Bill Goldberg," Schiavone told his TNT viewers, "a man we know absolutely nothing about. He is making his debut here and from the looks of him, he is very determined and looks very powerful."

If there are pro-wrestling history books, let them

record that Bill Goldberg's first televised bout was against Hugh Morris (a.k.a. "Humorous").

Goldberg's first move was, a forearm to Morris's head.

The new kid was down for a two-count early in the match but, later, he kicked out of Morris's signature move, "No Laughing Matter," a back flip made by the 300-pound wrestler off the top rope and right onto Goldberg, who was sprawled on his back in the middle of the ring. Goldberg did a standing back flip of his own later in the match and body-slammed Morris twice. That led WCW announcer Bobby Heenan to inject, "Hey, pretty agile for a big Goldberg!"

All right, it wasn't exactly a clinic, nor the most creative or technically-attractive match ever. Goldberg wrestled with little, or no, emotion. There was no "spear" (the football tackling move Goldberg later added to his devastating repertoire) but the raw rookie did get Morris up and down with a wobbly vertical suplex move (later named the "Jack Hammer") and pinned the veteran in 2:42. Goldberg turned to the camera and said "That's number one!"

"I WAS HORRIBLE!" Goldberg growled. "I'M STILL HORRIBLE! That first match was excruciating! I was more nervous than I think I've ever been in my life. You know, when you go out there, you want people to like you. If you force it, they're not gonna like you, so I just went out and did my job. Thanks to Hugh Morris, I got over pretty well in that first match and I started on my mystique right there. I came from nowhere. People didn't know who I was. That's what I wanted."

After his first bout, Goldberg blew off announcer "Mean" Gene Okerlund, who wanted a television interview. The next week, he pushed the camera aside and stalked off during a similar request. The die was cast. Bill Goldberg's wrestling persona was evolving. Fans were catching on. World Championship Wrestling was taking notice, but the man who was once known as one of college football's best "quote machines" was keeping mysteriously quiet, almost silent.

"It was my idea, first of all," Goldberg said. "If my character is based on realism, then I'm not going to go out there and give your stereotypical wrestling, screaming, yelling, interview. That's the one thing I didn't want to do, is be molded as a 'professional wrestler.' That's what separates me. It creates intrigue. People don't know much about you, so therefore, they are intrigued. They come to their own conclusions. I'm letting my work in the ring do my talking. When I talk, it's like my work in the ring. It's short, it's sweet, it's to the point and it has a purpose!"

THE ENTRANCE

Pro wrestling fans took to Bill Goldberg in a hurry. As his popularity grew, so did his undefeated record, and so did his marketability. Crowds began chanting his name long before the wrestler ever entered the arena. Goldberg remembers the first time he heard it.

"Washington, D.C. last year, during the hockey playoffs," he recalled. "I was standing, getting ready to go up on the stage for my entrance and I'm a bigger hockey fan than I am a football fan, and, to me, that was kind of like a hockey chant. It sent chills up and down my spine. It was just awesome! It's hard to describe. I was very honored."

Goldberg picked some pounding, ominous-sounding, almost dirge-like battle march music to announce his presence. Then, he teamed with WCW's pyrotechnic wizzes to create an entrance that makes Goldberg the focal point, the sizzling center-piece of what has to be the hottest entrance in all of sports.

PICTURE THIS! You are Goldberg's opponent. You stand in the ring waiting. His music begins. Fans chant and cheer. Focus shifts to the WCW stage at the end of the arena. The music pounds. A solitary figure appears ... black boots ... black knee wraps ... black briefs ... black-padded gloves and black elbow pads – warrior accessories on a frame that has been ripped and chiseled from years of intense exercise, weight training, and dedication to excellence. As you stand there and wait, the specimen steps from the darkness towards his mark on the metallic stage. Spotlights hit him. The man's neck builds like a mountain, starting at the shoulders and rippling its way north to his bald peak. He stops. Head bows. Huge arms dangle at his sides. There is peace, momentary peace.

Then, THE PYROTECHNICS FIRE OFF! The noise is startling! Sparkling stars of fire shoot from left and right, directly at the wrestler until he disappears in flashes of light and smoke. Moments later, the figure reappears, looking even more formidable, more forbidding, more ferocious. Goldberg has swallowed up the fire. He breathes out the smoke. He's a human dragon wearing black jockey shorts.

Schiavone put it best, "You can't even set the man on fire!"

Goldberg loves his incendiary entrance so much it hurts – literally. So, what's his inflammable secret?

"I douse myself with as much water as possible so that I don't spontaneously combust or ignite, but it is such a unique entrance, it's something that I can withstand because of its originality and how it sets itself off from everyone else's entrance," Goldberg said. "I endure through it because of the effect. It hurts! It burns for sure! It's kind of like sticking a big sparkler up your nose. I try

"You know, when you go out there, you want people to like you. If you force it, they're not gonna like you, so I, just went out and did my job.

not to breathe very much of it at all. Unfortunately, you have to weigh the ill effects of it!"

When Goldberg steps out of the fireworks, his glaring eyes rivet on the target – YOU! The face twists and contorts. The massive neck flexes. The powerful forearms rise from his sides as if to lift the already-standing throng to its tiptoes, like a muscle-bound evangelist raising his flock. The goateed mouth roars open wide, fireworks blast off behind him and Goldberg blasts out a primitive, guttural scream –

"ERRAAAAAAAAAAAAAAAAAHHHH!"

Tendons tense. Muscle fibers flex and activate. It's time to go to work. Goldberg's march to his roped office begins. Time to take care of business. With each heavy stride, there is a head slap, or a neck stretch, a spit, a slashing uppercut or a series of boxing combinations all designed to prepare this warrior for battle. Barely a few feet separate the wrestler from the fanatics who reach, claw and clamor to get close to him. The

In Colorado Springs, Goldberg got hit with a chair, hit in the head with a STOP sign, battled the entire "Flock," "Jack-Hammered" the gargantuan Reese and still managed to pin Raven in 4:58 to win the U.S. Heavyweight Championship. Goldberg got up off the canvas, contorted his face into a maniacal mask, stuck out his tongue and roared like a mad walrus. He grabbed the championship belt, held it up for all to see and looked right into the TNT camera and yelled, "IT'S MINE!" His career record was 75-0.

On July 6, 1998, Goldberg went home to the Georgia Dome in Atlanta. More than 40,000 fans were there and a national cable television audience was watching on TNT. Goldberg did away with Scott Hall in 5:35 to earn the right to meet the reigning champ and head bad guy, Hollywood Hogan, that same night. Less than a year on the wrestling circuit and Goldberg was getting his first shot at the WCW/nWo World Heavyweight title.

He conquered "Hollywood" faster than Spielberg. Goldberg used just 8:11 to win the unified championship and run his record to 108-0.

decibel level reaches the danger point. Distractions are all around, but Goldberg locks in on the task at hand, playing his role, pleasing the crowd and putting away his opponent as quickly, powerfully and dramatically as he can.

In Fargo, North Dakota, Goldberg made fast work of journeyman Barry Darsow, and broke the veteran's ribs with a "back-breaker" in the process.

The Atlanta crowd chanted "Gold-berg, Gold-berg" for a full three minutes until the *Nitro* show went off the air, and for several minutes more after that. Goldberg climbed up on the ropes, held the championship belts high, worked the Georgia Dome crowd, and realized he had found the "rush" that had been missing.

"It was like someone shot a lightning bolt through my body," Goldberg offered in

"Seventy-five percent of the people in the world think wrestling is fake," he said "Fifty percent of them think that they know it's fake. I put a bit of doubt in every one of those people's minds. That's my job!"

a reverential tone. "I wouldn't have wanted to be any other place in my life. It was a thrill to have all those people yelling for me. It was something I never got playing football. I guess it filled that void."

AH, THE SWEET SMELL OF SUCCESS!

WCW had found something, too — a new cash cow with which to stuff its already overflowing coffers! Goldberg's title bout with Hogan last July drew a 6.9 quarter-hour televi-sion rating, the highest ever for pro wrestling on cable. The replay of his October championship match with Diamond Dallas Page proved even better: a 7.2 rating, which made it the most-watched wrestling match ever televised on cable.

Goldberg's stock was taking off and his merchandise was moving out the door at an incredible rate. Goldberg action figures, sweatshirts, mugs, necklaces, jerseys, caps, collector cars, t-shirts, trading cards, posters, plaques, plates, blankets and boxer shorts were ringing up huge sales. His appearance with Kevin Nash last fall on QVC helped the cable shopping channel haul in more than half a million dollars from WCW merchandise sales in just one hour.

According to Michael Weber, WCW's director of marketing, "Goldberg is the top-selling product that we have going. He is the No. 1 individual selling product out there. He is a big part of the overall success that we are experiencing right now in licensing and retail merchandising."

A big part of the more than 200 million dollars that the WCW raked in in 1998 was from merchandise sales alone. All this money, exposure, recognition, celebrity, marketability and success came quickly for Goldberg. It still has the wrestler a bit surprised, yet surprisingly humble.

"Hey man, I'm no different than anybody else," Goldberg said in a matter-of-fact way. "I'm just on TV twice a week. It's flattering! It obviously helps my career, but there's nothing that's been done, or nothing that can be done, that will change how I am. It's flattering! It's embarrassing! I'm just happy to be in the position I am in, to be able to get the credit that I do. It doesn't mean I'm more special than anybody, it just means that I'm lucky."

Lucky to be extremely successful at a job he never really wanted. Goldberg's meteoric rise, though, has not come without sacrifices. You see, he never, ever, wanted to shave his chest and body hair. Now he does it, regularly, to get that super-smooth, high-definition, body-builder look. It may be necessary, but it sure ain't fun!

"I've cut myself many times," Goldberg said, and then laughed. "It just adds to my number of scars. It makes me look like a warrior. Going out there looking like Wolfman doesn't carry over too well."

He never, ever, ever wanted to perform wearing wrestling briefs. Now Goldberg's black "trunks" are his everyday work clothes! That wasn't supposed to happen!

"No, I did everything I could to get away from that," Goldberg said. "I wanted to wear a wrestling singlet, football pants, or something. I was digging for anything to not have to wear my underwear out there."

Minor sacrifices, I think you'll agree, when you stack them up against Goldberg's enormous professional, and monetary, success so far. He should feel luckiest that wrestling fans across America have taken to him and taken him in so quickly. They accepted him right away and bought in to his Neanderthal character. Lucky that WCW's brass picked up on the fan reaction and put Goldberg's career on a "smart" missile to the top of the profession. Fortunate that he has taken his opportunity and made the very most of it.

Goldberg says his connection with wrestling fans is based on a simple formula.

"Seventy-five percent of the people in the world think wrestling is fake," he said "Fifty percent of them think that they know it's fake. I put a bit of doubt in every one of those people's minds. That's my job!"

Goldberg goes to great lengths to create that doubt. He really, and truly, beats up lockers and dents doors with his bald head as part of his pre-bout ritual/psych session.

"It's quite similar to what I did to psych myself up for football," he said as if this was, somehow, normal. "I hit a couple lockers, butt the doors with my head and I'm ready to go. I just kind of get in the zone. That's what does it for me. I've got to go out there and be an intense character from the get-go, not just when I get in the ring and get hit! From the beginning on, from when the fans see me on, I HAVE GOT TO BE ON!"

You want real? Buck Martin, the V.P. of booking and events services at the Great Western Forum, got the true picture last summer in Los Angeles, when Goldberg was gearing up backstage for a WCW Cage match.

"Bill comes out and he's getting fired up, breathing heavy and pumping his chest out," Martin recalled. "Right when they announced his name, he turned and put his head into the steel-case fire door and put a dent in it that was probably about an inch deep and five inches in diameter. You see the strength and the girth of these doors, you can't believe that somebody human could do

something like that. You'd have to take a bat to put a dent in a door like that. That's just not normal!"

But it is real! So was the stun gun, or cattle prod, that intruder Scott Hall used to "zap" Goldberg on December 27, during his championship defense match against Kevin Nash at "Starrcade" in Washington, D.C. Goldberg was 173-0 going into that match, but due to the electrifying circumstances,

he got pinned, suffered the first loss of his career, and Nash walked away with the championship belts.

Goldberg knew he couldn't go undefeated forever, but the man hates to lose at anything.

He also hates to hear people question his profession, his athletic abilities, or those of his wrestling colleagues.

Goldberg understands that he is part athlete-part actor, but he is constantly seeking reality in the fantasy land of sports and entertainment.

So, whatever you do, if you run into Bill Goldberg, don't ask him if what he does is fake, because you may find out first-hand!

"My answer is, if you think it's fake, stand 10 feet away from me," Goldberg challenges, "and let me hit you with my tackle. If you can get up and brush it off and laugh, then it's fake. Not too many people have taken me up on that!"

Nor will they!

FLAIR:
14 Titles And Counting

By Blake Norton

On March 14, 1999, the most successful wrestler in the history of the sport won his 14th world title, almost 25 years after the plane crash that broke his back had doctors saying he'd never wrestle again.

Three weeks earlier, the "Nature Boy" had celebrated his 50th birthday. Ric Flair has dominated two full generations of main-event stars, and still manages to stay at the top, often facing stars half his age and matching up move for move. Steamboat, Race, Rhodes — all men who have fought and fallen to the Nature Boy, and hung up their boots long ago.

When Flair defeated Dusty Rhodes for his first world title on Sept. 17, 1981, the Hulk Hogan character that would ultimately be his only equal in terms of modern wrestling dominance hadn't even been created.

He lost the title to Harley Race on June 10, 1983, only to regain it on Nov. 24 at the first-ever "Starrcade." They swapped it again over two days on tour the following March. In the summer of 1984, Kerry Von Erich defeated Flair in Texas in an emotionally-charged match. Kerry had lost his brother shortly before the card. The reign was under three weeks long.

In 1985, Flair joined up with Tully Blanchard and Arn and Ole Anderson to form the first Four Horsemen. The heels took a strong grasp of the federation, feuding with Magnum T. A. and Dusty Rhodes. On July 26, 1986, Flair lost the title to Rhodes. Again, it was a short reign. After two weeks, the belt was back around the waist of Ric Flair, the most dominant champion the NWA had seen since Lou Thez. On Nov. 25, 1987, Ronnie Garvin won his only world championship from Flair, who picked it up for the sixth time in a rematch two months later at the fifth annual "Starrcade."

In 1989, Flair turned 40, and had a phenomenal series of matches with Ricky Steamboat. Ricky enjoyed a three-month reign (his only taste of world gold) between Feb. 20, 1989, and May 7, 1989. Sting joined the Horsemen at the end of that year, only to be ejected and beaten up. He spent several months on crutches going in to 1990, and made a huge comeback to win his first world title over Flair at the "Great American Bash" that summer. After the match, Sting

called the Nature Boy "the greatest of all time." Sting's reign lasted six months.

In 1991, Flair had disputes with management, who at the time wanted to tone down Flair's role in the company and asked him to take a major pay cut. After failing to come to terms, Flair jumped to the WWF that summer, while still the NWA world champion. He joined up with Curt Hennig, who had been forced out of the ring due to injury at "Summerslam."

Flair won his eighth world title at the "Royal Rumble" in January 1992 by outlasting 30 other men, last eliminating Hulk Hogan. Many say that it was the best "Rumble" of all time, and most put it down to the performance of 42-year-old Flair throughout the 60-minute event.

Having lost the strap to Randy Savage at "Wrestlemania VIII" on April 4, 1992, he won it back two days after "Summerslam," defeating the injured champion by way of his famed Figure Four Leglock. That October, he dropped the strap to Bret Hart in Canada (Hart's first world championship), and left the federation early the next year when Vince McMahon decided he no longer fit in the roster. They parted ways amicably,

with Flair doing the "loser leaves the company" job to Curt Hennig on *Raw* on Jan. 25, 1993.

As he returned to WCW, the question was "could Flair win his 10th world title?" It had never been done before, nor had anyone thought it possible. Flair had nine, two more than Harley Race's previous record of seven. Originally, the answer was to be no. WCW was going to phase him out. He did defeat Barry Windham for the NWA title at "Bash at the Beach '93," but at that time it was the secondary title in the company. Plans for Flair's future changed at the last minute when Sid, who was set to defeat Vader for the WCW championship and take up the role as No. 1 man in the federation at "Starrcade," got into a hotel room brawl with Arn Anderson. Sid was out of the picture, and Flair was the most obvious man to put in his place. He defeated the mammoth, dominant

Again the top man in the company, Flair was a runaway success, still boasting some of the best wrestling skills on the continent.

champion for his 10th strap, 10 years after he'd put away Race for his second.

Again the top man in the company, Flair was a runaway success, still boasting some of the best wrestling skills on the continent. He reignited his classic battles with Steamboat and defended against Vader before defeating WCW "International Champion" (the remains of the NWA title) Sting to unify the two heavyweight titles that had been floating around since the NWA withdrew from WCW. It was that summer that Hulk Hogan came

to the company. Flair went heel and put the "Hulkster" over cleanly in his first match for the company at "Bash at the Beach '94." Hogan and Jimmy Hart brought back many of the old 1980s WWF favorites, including Jim Duggan and the Honky Tonk Man, to supplement the rebirth of Hulkmania. Flair continued to put the champ over, rejuvenating Hogan's career, until "Halloween Havoc," where he did so for the last time in a "loser must retire" cage match.

He came back shortly after, reigniting a feud with Randy Savage. The following fall, he asked Sting to team up with him to take on "enemies" Arn Anderson and Brian Pillman, only for it to be a double-cross, which resulted in one of the many reincarnations of the Horsemen. At "Starrcade '95," Flair defeated Lex Luger and Sting to win the opportunity to face Randy Savage in the main event, ultimately unseating him for WCW's top title. He lost it three weeks later on *Nitro*, but came back to take it again at "Superbrawl VI" with the aid of Savage's real-life ex-

wife Elizabeth. On April 22, 1996, he put over The Giant, jobbing to the massive star after selling the whole match.

At the end of 1997, the Horsemen disbanded again when Curt Hennig, who replaced Arn Anderson, double-crossed the group in the "War Games." Flair was out for several weeks and made sporadic appearances on TV until Eric Bischoff decided he wanted the Horsemen back together, as WCW was losing the ratings war. The night he told Flair to return, Flair was at his son's wrestling tournament, and ended up being sued by WCW. In the fall of 1998, they finally came to semi-agreement, and the Horsemen came back on *Nitro* and began a long feud with Eric Bischoff. Flair lost to Bischoff at "Starrcade," but his son David defeated Bischoff on *Nitro* to win Ric control of WCW, and he's still acting president today. This scenario led to Hogan again feuding with Flair after he avenged Eric's loss to David by attacking Flair at "Souled Out" in January 1999.

On March 14, 1999, Flair's victory over Hulk Hogan gave him his 14th title. Proving once again that he can work the crowd as well as anyone, he has subtly turned fans against him. The fans who thought they were cheering for tradition, who thought they were cheering for wrestling pride, have been tricked by "Slick Ric" into hating him again all of a sudden, by way of the most subtle change in his mannerisms. As he slinks away from the fans, he looks once at the shiny gold belt on his shoulder, twice at the scornful faces peering down at him from the crowd, and gives a sly grin; he's home again. Flair is truly enjoying what may be his last reign at the top. Then again, this is Ric Flair we're talking about – 14 time champion of the world.

Flair is truly enjoying what may be his last reign at the top. Then again, this is Ric Flair we're talking about — 14-time champion of the world.

Nitro Girls

Wrestling's Dancing Queens

Chae

F or those who prematurely assumed that this would be 20 pages of worship and measurement facts – you're wrong. Fans already know that when they tune into TNT on Monday nights, their eyes will be fixated on the musical mirage of erotic salvation.

Imagine sitting at a private WCW roundtable, brainstorming strategic notions to prevent viewers from switching the channel during the commercial break. Eight centerfold beauties shaking their tootsie rolls in glossy Daisy Dukes may have been just what the wrestling world needed.

What are they wearing next? How many are coming out? Techno-style or bump-and-grind? The Nitro Girls have religiously maintained the carnal interest of eager wrestling fans worldwide.

Still eager to learn? Then we are about to reveal the answers to questions that have long lurked in your minds about the World Championship Wrestling's show stealers!

While the competition continued to push the envelope with

content suitable for an audience craving mature, late-night hardcore, Eric Bischoff conceived a master plan that would offer a "socially correct" working female portrayal. Not that we feel "other" females of the industry do not work as hard as the Nitro Girls – we know how hard it can be when the hooks of a new bra won't open with one hand – but WCW has offered its fans the freedom of choice and variation with a conservative glamour bonanza.

The marriage of Nitro Girl leader Kimberly Page to WCW superstar Diamond Dallas Page has already been exposed to the public. Although life may be smoochie-boochie at home, the game faces are on in the locker room. Page conducts his business with fellow wrestlers, while Kimberly preps the troupe for seven or more exhausting renditions during a three-hour live show. The atmosphere becomes strictly professional with the stern intention of getting the job done.

"The girls represent a wide ethnic and cultural diversity,"

explained team captain Kimberly. "We're breaking new ground, and before you know it, we'll be bigger than the Dallas Cowboys cheerleaders!"

While most fans only witness the spandex sporting dance sequences with occasional tempting gyrations, there are questions that have been left unanswered ... until now! Nitro Girls EXPOSED? You be the judge!

The Nitro Girls have religiously maintained the carnal interest of eager wrestling fans worldwide.

Contractually, the Nitro Girls all work with the same deal, which was recently re-signed for an extended three-year period. The only thing that changes with their weekly routines is the city and the hotel. Mondays and Tuesdays are dedicated to travel; Wednesdays are grueling hours of rehearsals; Thursdays are ballet classes; and whatever days and times are left over are usually filled with time at the gym, tanning salon, manicures or personal appearances at venues selling advance tickets for upcoming Nitro events.

"We practically have no social lives," explained an almost mentally extinguished Fyre, "because everything we do revolves around the show." The constant and irregular schedules have taken its toll on the girls. "Sometimes the only real sleep I get is on the plane," said a jet-lagged Chae. "People don't know how hard we work. We are on the road as much as the

wrestlers."

With time constraints on both their personal and professional lives, it is almost impossible to reserve an appointment in any non-affiliated projects. WCW has recently discussed the production of exclusive Nitro Girl merchandise, which would commit the girls to more sessions than originally scheduled. The merchandise would include individual and group calendars, posters, fitness videos and action figures. Another event planned in their yearly itinerary is the WCW Bruise Cruise, which sets sail in mid-May. How many male wrestling fans do you think attend these cruises in hopes of recreating a scene from *Titanic* with a Nitro Girl?

Enter the burn from the celebrity spotlight, yet exit the life you once lived. Not an easy task at all, especially when WCW bookers have started discussing the addition of Nitro

"We practically have no social lives, because everything we do revolves around the show." -- Fyre

Girls into the storylines. In a recent edition of Nitro, Kimberly was brutally attacked and thrown from a moving vehicle by Big Poppa Pump. This naturally raised the gates on the acting abilities of the girls, who expressed concern over their fallen leader. "It should be fun," said an ecstatic Spice. "Our involvement will finally give us speaking roles, but none of them will lead into any of the girls breaking off from the group or managing a wrestler." Tygress added, "We want our roles to be maintained as Nitro Girls, and not cross the line into being recognized as a valet."

Have there been offers to any of the Nitro Girls that would require them to quit the team and pursue other endeavors? "Whenever there are attractive females in the public eye, everyone has an offer lined up for you," explained the 5'10" former swimsuit model Whisper. "They want you to be on the cover of this and endorse that, but in the end, they all end up as one-shot deals. I'm a Nitro Girl. The other girls are my family, friends and consultants. There is a

"Our involvement (in WCW storylines) will finally give us speaking roles, but none of them will lead into any of the girls breaking off from the group..."

-- Spice

loyalty and bond between us that other offers can never guarantee."

MTV had expressed interest in obtaining the services of Whisper last year, after the girls had appeared on the hit dating show *Singled Out*. There was talk of offering Whisper her own romance show on the MTV network in hopes that her wrestling audience would follow. There was also talk of numerous muscle and fitness magazines that wanted to acquire Chae's modeling services for promotional advertisements.

As far as new additions to the fleet, you'd have a better chance at hitting the devil with a snowball in Hell. All Nitro Girls are opposed to bringing in new members. As it is, the eight girls were carefully selected through recommendations rather than auditions. "There are so many girls who want to be Nitro Girls, but it is usually for all the wrong reasons," testified leader and recruiting officer Kimberly. "It is really hard to find a complete stranger and expect the loyalty and commitment that is needed for this alliance. Practically all the girls we have now were recommended through previous projects. Look at the resumes. Both AC and Chae were Atlanta Falcons cheerleaders. What a coincidence, huh?"

"Adding new girls to the group usually throws us off," said Fyre. "We have to take time and train them in the old steps and routines so that they can pick up the new ones. Time is usually a luxury we don't have, and it always ends up bringing us back to stage one." The newest and final member of the group, Storm, says that she was really pressured when first joining the team because she did not want to be responsible for breaking their momentum. "There were times that I thought twice about what I was doing," Storm said. "I didn't want to hold them back from what they had to do. One day, Amy pulls me aside and says, 'It's not personal. We'll keep doing this until you learn it.' The girls really tried to make it as easy as possible for me. They even offered for me to stay at their houses during the weekends so we could practice as much as possible." Mistakes happen and when they do, the girls agree on one motto: "There's always next Monday!"

You seem to know a lot about the Nitro Girls now. But there is still that one question that haunts you. That one voice that says, "This better not be over until they answer The Question!" Do the Nitro Girls have any personal relationships with the wrestlers? The answer is ... No!

Before the creation of the Nitro Girls, Eric Bishoff repeatedly demanded a verbal agreement from Kimberly Page that she would supervise and carry out the responsibility of restricting any relations that would conflict with the work code of her girls and his boys. When contracts were issued, a strict clause was agreed upon and signed by all girls stating that any relations that affected business would lead to immediate termination.

Relationships between Nitro Girls and wrestlers are strictly professional. "They're all like my big brothers" said the bubbly AC. "Even after the shows, if they feel that someone is bothering us a little too much, 'big brother' steps in for the save."

Gorgeous George

WCW

Can't wait for action!

Elizabeth
WCW

Feeling lucky
today?

bombshells bombshells

Torrie Wilson
WCW
Too Hot for David?

Al Snow

Fed: WWF
Age: 35
Physical: 6'0", 230 lbs
Style(s): Brawler
Highest Accolade: WWF Hardcore
Champion

Jerry Lawler

Fed: WWF
Age: 49
Physical: 6'0", 240 lbs
Style(s): Brawler
Highest Accolade: AWA/WCCW Heavyweight Champion

The King of What!?!

gangrel
Fresh WWF talent

shawn michaels

Wrestler of the '90s

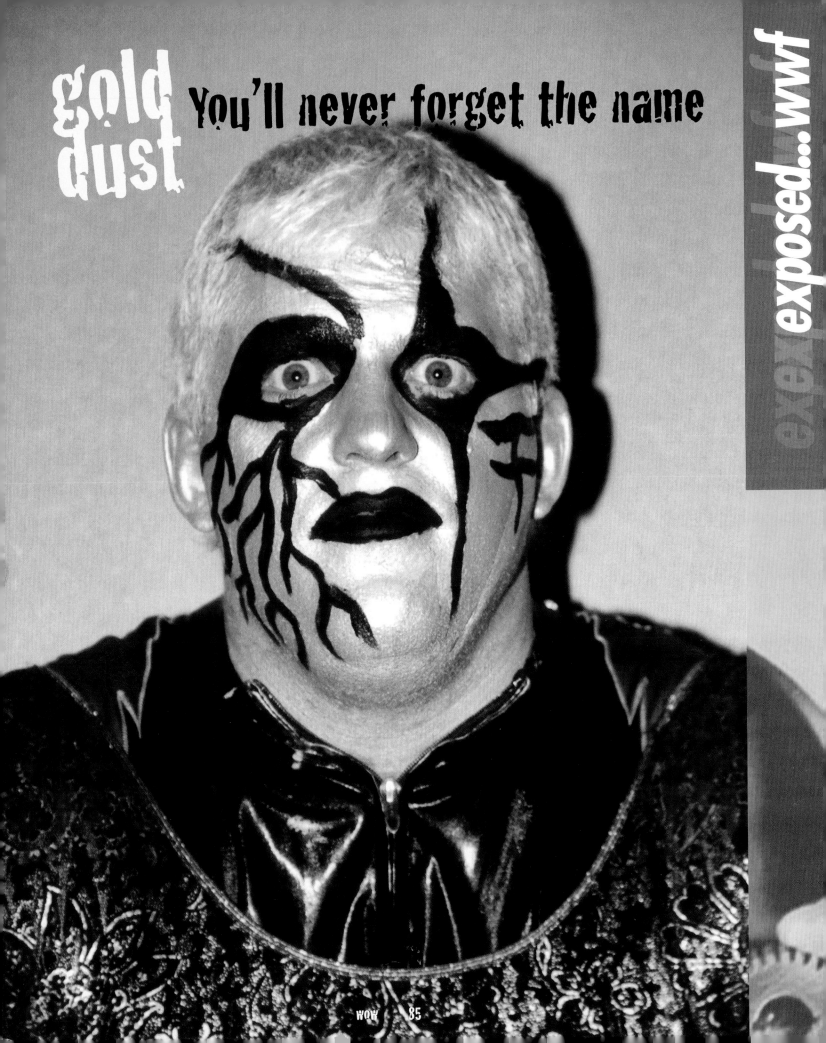

gold dust You'll never forget the name

exposed....wwf

edge Creature of the Night

THE ROC[K] IS COCKED LOCKED & LOAD[ED]

Dangerous & Deadly!

Ken Shamrock

Fed: WWF
Age: 35
Physical: 6'1", 235 lbs
Style(s): Submission Holds
Highest Accolade: Intercontinental Champion, Tag Team Champion (w/Big Boss Man)

The Godfather

Fed: WWF
Physical: 6'6", 320 lbs
Style(s): Brawler
Highest Accolade: Intercontinental Champion

Pimpin' Ain't Easy!

Finally Seen the Light?

The Brood:
Christian,
Edge &
Gangrel

Blue Meanie

Fed: WWF
Physical: 6'1", 292 lbs
Style(s): Brawler
Highest Accolade: Moderate success in the Intercontinental Division

AUSTIN 3:1

J.O.B. squad
1-2-3

Back in Blue

Val Venis

Fed: WWF
Physical: 6'2", 240 lbs
Style(s): Mat Wrestler
Highest Accolade: Intercontinental Champion

XXX Matwork

Can You Smell What the Sock is Cookin'?

Mankind

Fed: WWF
Age: 34
Physical: 6'2", 287 lbs
Style(s): Brawler
Highest Accolade: 2-time Tag Team
Champion, 2-time Federation
Champion

Kane

Fed: WWF
Physical: 7'0", 326 lbs
Style(s): Power Moves, Brawler
Highest Accolade: Federation
Champion, 3-time Tag Team
Champion

What Will He Do Next?

The Undertaker

Fed: WWF
Age: 34
Physical: 6'10", 332 lbs.
Style(s): Brawler/High Flyer
Highest Accolade: WWF World Champion

Road Dogg

Fed: WWF
Age: n/a
Physical: 6'2", 260 lbs.
Style(s): Brawler
Highest Accolade: WWF
Intercontinental Champion

24 7 365 d-generation-x 69

WOW 95

D'Lo Brown

Fed: WWF
Age: n/a
Physical: 6'2", 280 lbs.
Style(s): Mat Wrestler/High Flyer
Highest Accolade: WWF European Champion

marc mero

Will he ever get BADD again?

The Rock

the rock   '98

"This Ain't Sing-Along."

The Rock rises to the top of the sports entertainment business

His right eyebrow rises high into his forehead while his millions and millions of fans around the world watch with great anticipation.

What will he say? What will he do?

The red light is beaming brightly. He looks straight into the camera and yells, "Do You Smeeeellllll ..."

Then he pauses.

The live crowd finishes his thought, loud and clear.

Arrogantly, he tells the audience, "This ain't sing-along."

He continues, "... What The Rock Is Cooking?"

The fans erupt.

The Rock's demeanor and mat skills have made him one of the hottest commodities in professional wrestling.

If you ask him, and even if you don't, he confidently says in the third person, "The Rock is the most electrifying man in sports entertainment today!"

It's hard to argue the point.

In just three years, The Rock has become a household name in the wrestling world, winning the WWF Intercontinental Title twice and the WWF heavyweight belt three times. He's been featured in numerous newspapers and magazines and on TV shows, including a guest appearance on *That '70s Show.*

The Rock boasted, "Everybody loves The Rock. Everybody wants a piece of The Rock. Who wouldn't? I guaran-damn-tee you I am the greatest sports entertainer today. The Rock is a very lucky man, I'll be the first to admit that. After coming out of the University of Miami in 1995, The Rock got into wrestling in 1996, and a lot of great things have happened to The Rock."

He added, "But let's not forget how hard The Rock works. The Rock takes great pride in outworking everyone in the ring and out of the ring."

The Rock is an innovator. He loves to call his own match, grabbing the headset from Michael Cole or Jim Ross during a heated battle to lend some on-hand insight. During the WWF pay-per-view "Backlash" in April, he debuted The Rock Cam, taking the television camera from the cameraman and calling his actions while working the TV equipment.

"The Rock also takes extreme pride in being creative in what he does, in the words he speaks in interviews and the matches he has in the ring," he said.

Fans love to listen to The Rock. Fans enjoy watching him wrestle.

"The Rock will be the first one to say what The Rock does is strictly entertainment. It's called sports entertainment, but to The Rock it's

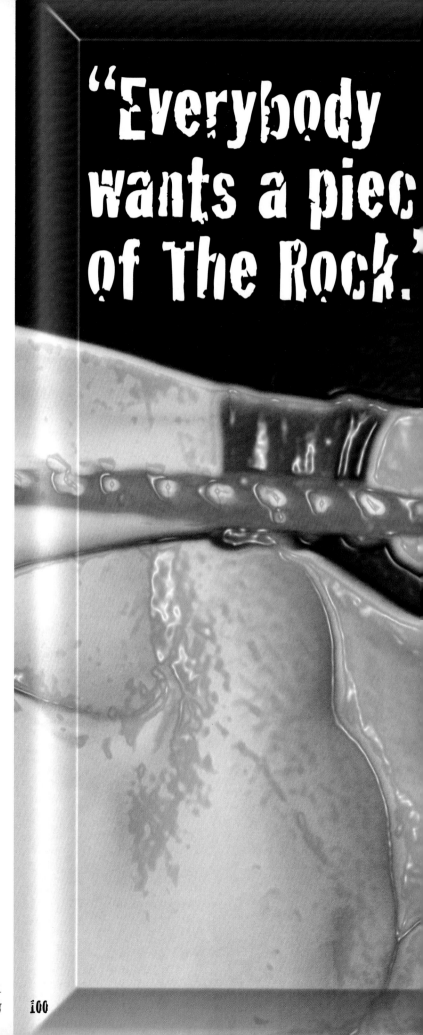

"Everybody wants a piec of The Rock."

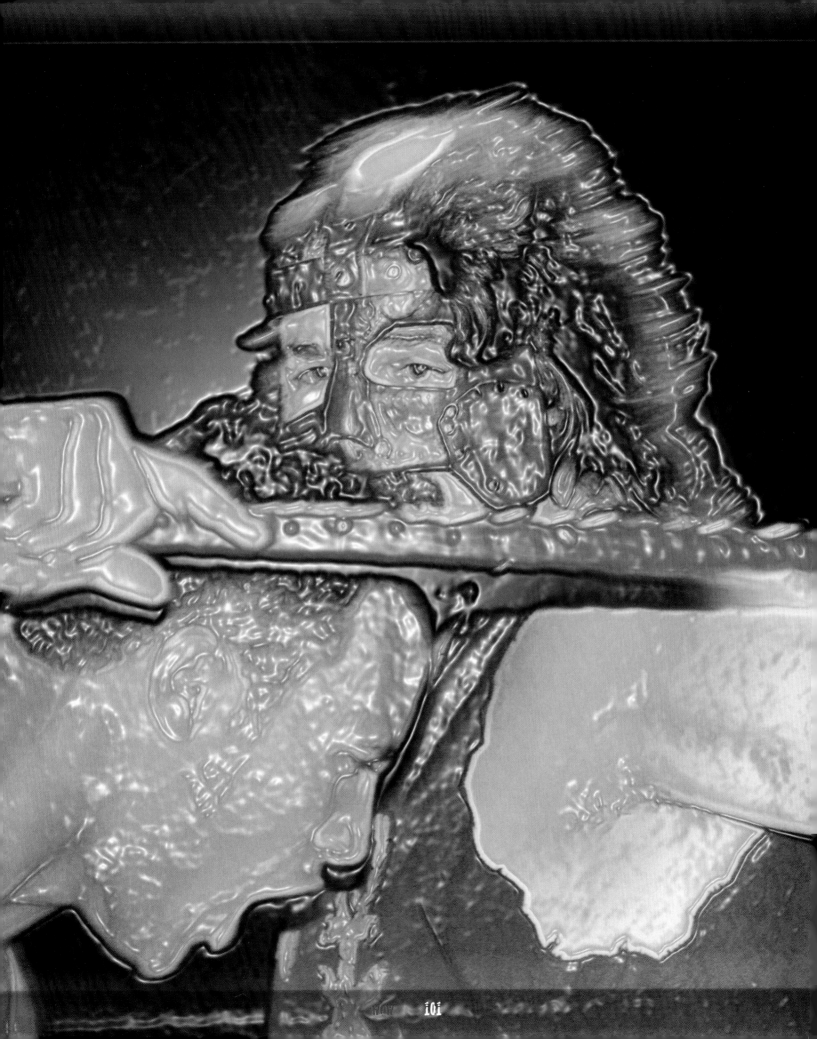

entertainment first. The Rock's No.1 priority is to entertain the millions and millions of The Rock fans, and that's exactly what The Rock does, and quite frankly, nobody does it better."

The Rock electrifies the crowd night in and night out.

The Rock's family tree lists some outstanding wrestling history: his father Rocky Johnson, his grandfather High Chief Peter Maivia, and his uncles Afa and Sica the Wild Samoan and Jimmy Superfly Snuka.

One glaring difference between today's wrestlers and the wrestlers of yesterday is their open attitude about the business. Rocky Johnson would never tell someone outside the family that the matches were pre-determined.

But The Rock will be the first one to say that because he is leading the pack in saying what we do is complete entertainment, pre-determined entertainment.

"It's an action adventure show; it's a live show; it's a physical play; it's a physical soap opera full of storylines," The Rock said. "No one is trying to pull the wool over anyone's eyes about professional wrestling."

When The Rock wrestles in Florida, he needs plenty of comp tickets for family and friends. They sit ringside, enjoying the action and supporting their No.1 grappler.

"All I can say, wrestling is very different now," said Ata Johnson, The Rock's mom and High Chief Peter Maivia's daughter. "Every match my father wrestled was an experience, and I enjoyed it. All the years watching my husband wrestle, every match was also an experience, and I enjoyed it."

But no matter how big or how old, Dwayne Johnson is still Ata Johnson's little boy.

"Watching my son wrestle, I don't know how to describe it. It is very, very different because you just have that motherly instinct thinking he is going to get hurt. I know he can take care of himself, and I know he is talented, but you still think that."

She continued, "So, I'll sit at ringside and hold his wife's hand, or she'll hold mine, and hope he wins every match he gets into."

Ata Johnson remembers good guy Rocky Maivia returning home to wrestle his first match at the Miami Arena. Still green, he faced Florida State University grad Ron Simmons, a.k.a. Faarooq. The UM-rooting crowd celebrated as Maivia pinned Faarooq.

"It gave me goose bumps," Ata Johnson said. "I found myself really getting carried away with the fans, jumping up on the chairs and enjoying it. I wish my husband had been there to see the way he wrestled that night."

Rocky Johnson made many trips to watch his son compete in the ring, stopping backstage to visit the new wrestlers and some of his old friends working for the WWF like Tony Garea.

When Dwayne Johnson played college football, Rocky and Ata Johnson traveled from their home in Tampa to all of the UM football team's home games in the Orange Bowl.

"Football was in his heart, and that was also in our heart," Ata Johnson said, "but his dad and I always had it in the back of our minds, wrestling is in there somewhere, and it did come out."

"Pro wrestling ... it's in my blood," The Rock said.

The Rock/Dwayne Johnson took a page from his football playing days with the University of Miami and parlayed that into a very successful career move. Johnson was a member of the Hurricanes from 1991-94.

The transformation of Johnson from Rocky Maivia (a babyface) to The Rock (a heel) occurred in August 1997, when he decided no more Mr. Nice Guy.

"I tried to do everything to please the fans – shake hands, sign autographs – and what did it get me?" said Johnson, 26. "I'll tell ya. Fans would chant, 'Rocky Sucks! Rocky Sucks,' and hold up signs, 'Die Rocky Die!' I just get tired of not being appreciated by the fans."

So, Maivia changed. Within two years, the WWF gave birth to a cocky son-of-a-gun called The Rock.

The Rock then made a surprise move by joining the Nation of Domination led by his wrestling rival Faarooq, 40, a former two-time All-American who had his football jersey retired at Florida State.

"Joining the Nation of Domination gave me the ability to express myself," The Rock said. "Rocky Maivia really wasn't Dwayne Johnson. I would hear the vulgar comments from fans, and Rocky Maivia could not respond to that. I'd have to wear a smile on my face. It's not like that in real life. Now, if I want to smile, I smile, and if I don't want to smile, I don't. Like it or not, it's a breath of fresh air just being myself."

You just knew a team with Seminoles and 'Canes could not co-exist. It wasn't long before The Rock took charge of the Nation and ousted Faarooq. Eventually, The Rock set his own trail, ridding himself of D'Lo Brown, former Olympic powerlifter Mark Henry and The Godfather.

The Rock is arrogant, cocky and successful. A member of the 1991 national champion Hurricanes, he literally disrespects everybody, especially if you try to cross his path.

"With Coach Jimmy Johnson and Coach Dennis Erickson at UM, there was a brash style and a swagger that you had, and you made sure everyone knew it," The Rock said. "I'm not knocking the players today, but there was an amount of respect always given to us. If opponents didn't realize it, you damn sure taught them."

With this newfound attitude in the ring, an attitude reminiscent of those national champion Hurricanes teams, The Rock

● ●

"The Rock has done all he can to remain a heel. Having the cheers of the crowd has never been something that The Rock has desired. The Rock would love to always be the most hated man in sports entertainment."

● ●

captured the WWF Intercontinental Championship for the second time in his three-year career. In December 1997, then-champion Austin just handed the belt to him.

"Stone Cold was tired of getting his butt whipped," The Rock said, "so he just handed the belt over. I don't blame him."

The Rock claimed to be the People's Champ, mocking the crowd's disdain toward him. When fans began cheering The Rock and his signature move, The People's Elbow, he once again turned on them. The Rock sided with hated WWF owner Vince McMahon Jr. and his corporate honchos.

Another smart move. The Rock, with the backing of the corporation, won the WWF Heavyweight Championship in a tournament during the WWF pay-per-view "Survivor Series" in November.

The Rock defeated three of the toughest grapplers in the WWF: former Ultimate Fighting Champion Ken Shamrock, The Undertaker and Mankind. In the final, McMahon Jr. made

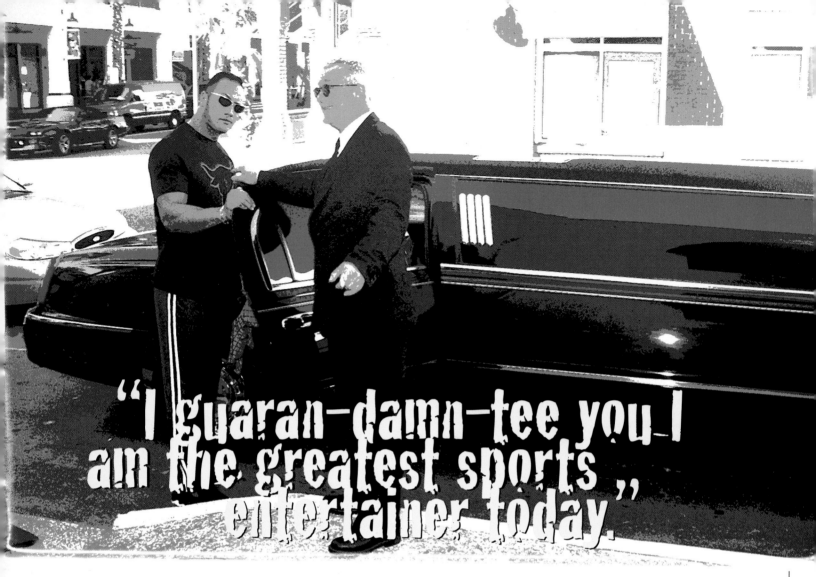

"I guaran-damn-tee you I am the greatest sports entertainer today."

the timekeeper ring the bell, claiming Mankind submitted to The Rock's version of the Sharpshooter, but Mankind never said, "I quit."

A happy McMahon Jr. and an equally pleased Shane McMahon celebrated vigorously and presented the world title to The Rock . The Rock was the world champion after less than three years in the biz.

"They can all say what they want," The Rock said. "You can't dictate to me what to do. The fact of the matter is you can't impeach me. I am not your President. I am not the People's Champion. I am the Corporate Champion."

Even with his bad boy image, he has built a strong allegiance of fans. There are some that still boo him, but more cheer him. It reflects the status of pro wrestling today.

The Rock is not shy. He speaks his mind, developing some of the marquee catch phrases today like, "Can you smell what The Rock is cooking?" "Know your role, and shut your mouth, you jabroni," and, "I can guaran-damn-tee it."

Many pro athletes and radio personalities are using The Rock's lines. It was no different in college.

When reporters needed a quote, a good quote, after a University of Miami football game, they scurried to Dwayne Johnson's locker. He knew what to say and how to say it.

"He has developed to be one heck of an entertainer," said Jay Rokeach, the longtime public address announcer for the University of Miami and a big wrestling fan. "Everybody loves the Corporate Elbow, and everybody loves the Corporate Eyebrow. He is somebody Hurricanes fans can be proud of."

Dwayne Johnson began playing football his junior year of high school after moving to Pennsylvania from Hawaii. A powerful kid who bench-pressed 415 pounds, it didn't take long for him to make an impact. *USA Today* ranked him the eighth-best player in the state his high school senior season. He caught the attention of the coaching staff at the University of Miami, and they inked him to a scholarship.

Injuries stymied Johnson's playing days at the University of Miami. A defensive tackle, he tore his left shoulder and sat out his first season as a redshirt. By his senior season, Johnson looked to shine, but instead battled back problems.

"I played in tremendous pain all year," said Johnson, a member of Coach Erickson's first and last UM teams. I should have been smarter and taken a couple of weeks off rather than two days, but that's hindsight.

"Miami is an intense football program, and I wanted to come back quick. It was my senior year."

Johnson totaled seven pressures and 27 tackles (19 assists, seven solo), including five against Pittsburgh. That followed a season in which he amassed 34 tackles and two sacks, including one on FSU quarterback and Heisman Trophy winner Charlie Ward.

Still, Johnson capped his college legacy with a degree in criminology and a couple of rings, one for winning a national title and the other for marrying his college sweetheart, Dani Garcia.

"Football has provided a lot of opportunities for me," Johnson said. "I was able to get a scholarship and earn a college degree. I met my wife, and I also had a chance to play pro football."

After the 1994 season, Johnson signed with the Calgary Stampeders in the Canadian Football League. He played one season on a Stampeders team that featured current Buffalo Bills quarterback Doug Flutie. After that, he opted to concentrate solely on pro wrestling.

A confident young man, Johnson always believed in himself, whether he was crashing through an offensive lineman, tackling the books or as a freshman courting his future wife, a senior who rowed for the university's crew team.

Garcia graduated in 1991 with a degree in international finance and marketing.

So what's it like to be married to "The Most Electrifying Man In Sports Entertainment" today? "It's not as wild as many people think," Garcia said. "When The Rock comes home, he is my husband. He is Dwayne Johnson. There is a lot more excitement when we go out. He is easily recognizable."

The Rock does his homework at home, symbolic of his playing days with the 'Canes.

"When he used to play football, we used to watch the Hurricane games afterward and discuss them and analyze them for what things he needs to do," Garcia said. "We do the same thing now, but we just do it when we watch the wrestling match-

es — what we like and what we didn't like. We just adjusted and adapted to it."

Garcia knows Johnson is a tremendous athlete. She played sports all her life, including track and rowing. She first set eyes on Johnson in the weight room at UM.

"I saw this fantastic looking man, and I said, 'Who is

> **That followed a season in which he amassed 34 tackles and two sacks, including one on FSU quarterback and Heisman Trophy winner Charlie Ward.**

that?' " Garcia said, chuckling. "He was so unique looking. After that we happened to meet at a club where many of the UM athletes hung out. Now, we work out together."

Garcia knew a little something about wrestling, so it wasn't a complete shock to her when he explained what his father, grandfather, uncles and cousins did for a living.

"It was a big eye-opener for me because I had never watched it before," she admitted. "I recognized a couple of names, Jimmy Superfly Snuka and Hulk Hogan, but it's been a great learning experience for me, especially when the family gets together, and we pull out the tapes, and we would watch his father wrestle. It was fantastic."

Now, you can't keep Garcia away.

"I love it. Everyone I know, we talk about wrestling."

A South Florida resident, The Rock is moving from Kendall, an unincorporated area of Miami-Dade County, roughly 30 miles north to Davie, a city west of Fort Lauderdale, with his wife.

"The Rock is coming to Davie with his better half. We're building a lavish house there, and we are going to make Davie our new home."

The WWF is in the midst of an all-out ratings war on Monday night. Not only does it battle *Monday Night Football* in the fall and other programming on the major networks, but its biggest rival is

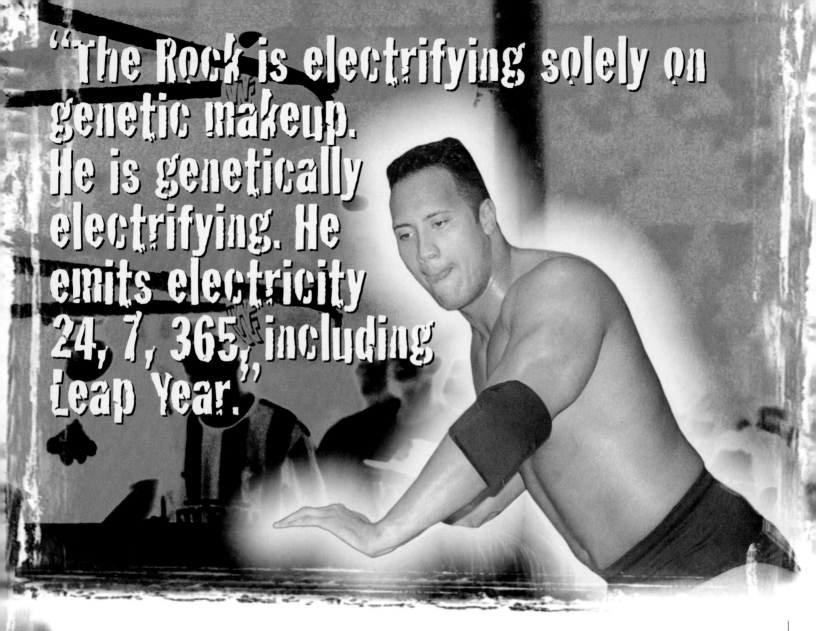

"The Rock is electrifying solely on genetic makeup. He is genetically electrifying. He emits electricity 24, 7, 365, including Leap Year."

World Championship Wrestling's Monday Nitro. The WWF's change has resulted in higher ratings against its competitors on Monday nights.

The WWF show on cable's USA Network is winning the ratings war on Monday nights against WCW in part because approximately 1.2 million of its total viewers each week are teenagers. WCW draws 3 million to 5 million total viewers a week, with roughly 475,000 of them teenagers.

The WWF is a little bit sexual, a little bit crude and a little bit vulgar on Monday nights, especially after 10 p.m. (EST). No bones about it, the *Raw Is War* show has a TV-14 rating.

"Absolutely, the parents should monitor what the kids are watching," The Rock said. "The WWF has weekend shows Saturday and Sunday that kids can watch. Monday nights are essentially for adults, but I know a lot of kids watch it, so what parents should do is monitor that show. The parents are the ones

allowing their kids to watch the WWF Monday nights. The parents are the ones allowing their children to purchase the Stone Cold Steve Austin finger and DX Suck It items in stores or at concession stands. What the kids do is up to the parents.

"The content of our Monday night show is adult oriented," The Rock said. "Take it for what it's worth. It's sports entertainment at its finest. The WWF personifies attitude. We are edgy, sometimes over the edge. More times than not we hit, and sometimes we miss with storylines. I definitely say parents go ahead and monitor what your kids are watching Monday nights because *Monday Night Raw* can be very racy and sexual."

The Rock added, "But I will still pitch family entertainment with the WWF programs Saturday morning, Sunday morning, Sunday night and even *Monday Night Raw*. If you turn to any other station, including your HBOs and other pay channels, you are going to see 100 times worse."

"I played in tremendous pain all year.

8:30

Stone Cold Steve Austin

The Evolution of a Superstar

The glass shatters. The crowd gets on its feet.

Walking down the ramp is perhaps the most identifiable athlete in pro wrestling history.

During the past two years, "Stone Cold" Steve Austin has taken the World Wrestling Federation and professional wrestling in general to a level never thought possible. Who would have thought seven years ago – when the wrestling industry was all but dead – that a guy who at the time was struggling to hold a job would turn it all around?

Austin has done for his sport what only one other man can say he has done – take pro wrestling to a whole new level.

Only Hulk Hogan in the mid-1980s had the right mix of charisma and talent to single-handedly bring back what once was a dying form of entertainment. For that alone, Austin will go down in wrestling history as one of the greatest performers to step through the ropes.

Before going on about "Stone Cold," it's important to reflect on the era when he was new to the sport and struggling to get an identity and role that was right for him. Just like all other pro wrestlers, Austin struggled in the independent ranks for years. When he finally made it to the big time in World Championship Wrestling, he had a hard time becoming the superstar he is considered today. He was given the gimmick of "Stunning" Steve Austin, a long-haired pretty boy much like Shawn Michaels. Needless to say, that role did not fit Austin's style. He was then paired with his friend (Brian Pillman), and they became the "Hollywood Blondes." That gimmick ultimately ran its course, and Austin once again searched for something else.

After a somewhat short stint with WCW, Austin was released due to an injury. After a short time with ECW, Austin finally landed the job that would make him the world-famous wrestler he is today. He was brought into the World Wrestling Federation and utilized immediately. He was known as the Ringmaster and given the Million-Dollar Belt, which was pos-

sessed by his manager at the time, Ted DiBiase.

It wasn't until about a year later that it all started to come together. June 23, 1996, is the day that "Stone Cold" Steve Austin was born. After winning the "King of the Ring" tournament by pinning Jake Roberts, Austin delivered the speech that would change his life forever. While accepting his crown for winning the tournament, he for the first time said those eight words, "Austin 3:16 says I just whupped your ass." At that moment, pro wrestling as fans knew it changed.

The surprise of Austin winning the "King of the Ring" was a master plan that Austin and Vince McMahon thought up only about a month ahead of time.

Austin went to McMahon and suggested a gimmick change more suited to his style. The men collaborated and came up with "Stone Cold," and the rest is history.

These days you can't turn around without seeing a "Stone Cold" something or other. The marketing skills of McMahon and everyone working for him have been nothing short of phenomenal during the past few months. The WWF is now reaping the benefits of its amazing booking and creative teams that make possible what you see on television every week. From the great success of the Rock to Mankind, Degeneration X and the recent corporate team, the WWF has countless success stories, none of which compare to the man they call the Rattlesnake.

Austin's rise to fame is something that never could have been predicted. It is something that comes around once in a lifetime, and that is why his story is so special. There will never be another "Stone Cold" Steve Austin, so make sure to enjoy him while he is still around, because no matter how many people try to copy him, they will never even come close to the man himself.

Debra McMichael
wwf

Can she handle her tag-team partners?

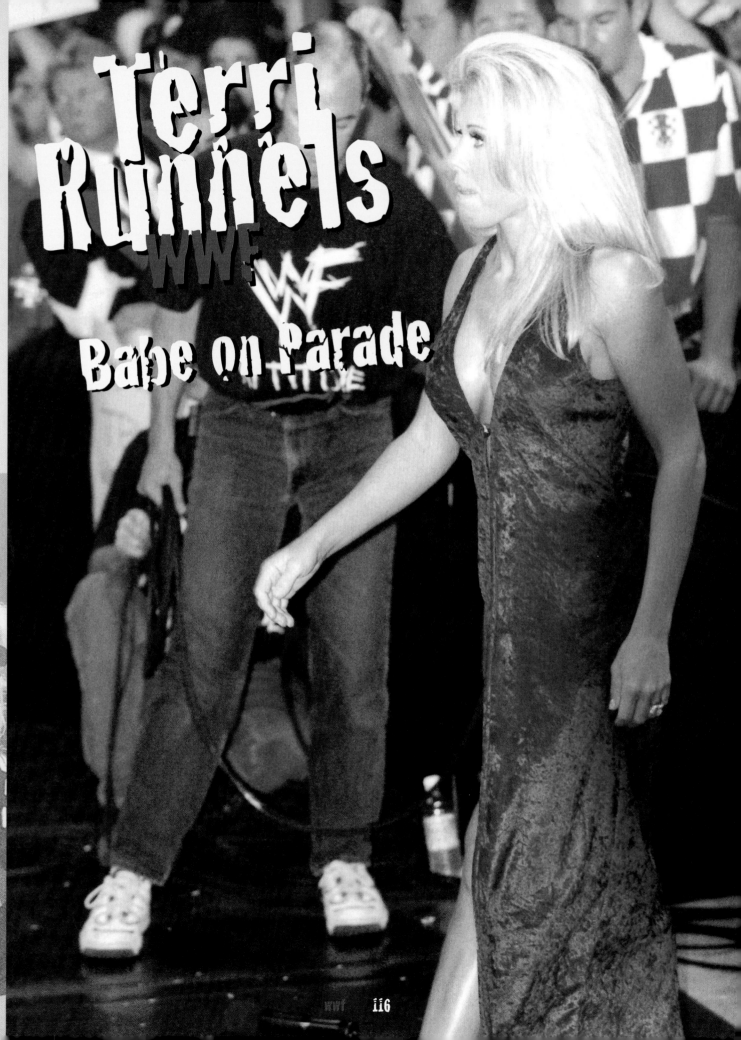

Terri Runnels

WWF

Babe on Parade

Jacqueline

wwf
On top of the World!

Chyna
wwf
You want me?
Come and
get some!

118

Luna
wwf
I'm just a little crazy today!

bombshells bombshells

Test Your WIQ

Wrestling Trivia Challenge

By Donny Laible

Think you're an expert on all things wrestling? Give your Wrestling Intelligence Quotient a spin at the following trivia and find out how high your WIQ is.

Choose the right answer for each of the following questions:

1. What current WWF superstar formerly competed as one half of manager Al Costello's Fabulous Kangaroos tag team?
A. "Too Hot" Scott Taylor
B. Al Snow
C. Billy Gunn

2. While competing for Smoky Mountain Wrestling, which wrestler didn't D'Lo Brown manage and/or team with?
A. New Jack
B. Mustafa
C. Kareem Muhammad

3. When he co-held his first of two ECW tag titles, who was Taz's partner?
A. Kevin Sullivan
B. Mikey Whipwreck
C. Johnny Hotbody

4. What American defeated Japan's Antonio Inoki in 1983 en route to being the first ever IWGP champion?
A. Scott Norton
B. Stan Hansen
C. Hulk Hogan

5. What current WCW superstar won the promotion's light heavyweight (now cruiserweight) belt in 1992 under the guise of Scotty Flamingo?
A. Raven
B. Saturn
C. Chris Jericho

6. Barry Windham claimed WCW's Television championship from what current WWF main eventer?
A. Mankind
B. Steve Austin
C. Road Warrior Hawk

7. During his college basketball career, Big Sexy Kevin Nash played at what university?
A. Syracuse
B. Arizona State
C. Tennessee-Knoxville

8. In his pre-Public Enemy days, Flyboy Rocco Rock flew off turnbuckles as what identity?
A. Amazing Zuma
B. Black Tiger
C. Cheetah Kid

9. What wrestler experienced the shortest reign as WWF champion?
A. Stan Stasiak
B. Ivan Koloff
C. Iron Sheik

10. While touring with the NWA, Mean Mark Callous was managed by:
A. Paul E. Dangerously
B. Jim Cornette
C. Harley Race

Answers: 1.B 2.C 3.A 4.C 5.A 6.B 7.C 8.C 9.A 10.A

Match the title to the wrestler who won it. Keep in mind that all titles are listed as they were named:

1. WWF InterContinental
2. AWA Heavyweight
3. WCW Tag Team
4. NWA National
5. NWA Heavyweight
6. Florida State
7. UWF Television
8. Central States
9. Smoky Mountain Wrestling
10. WWC Caribbean
11. WWF Tag Team
12. NWA Western States Heritage
13. Canadian Television
14. Pacific Northwest Tag Team

A. Kevin Sullivan
B. Bruiser Brody
C. Buddy Rose & Colonel DeBeers
D. Tracey Smothers
E. Paul Orndorff
F. Ken Patera
G. Scott Hall
H. Masa Saito
I. Ron Garvin
J. Shane Douglas
K. Arn Anderson & Paul Roma
L. Angelo Mosca Jr.
M. Larry Zbyszko
N. Yukon Lumberjacks

Answers: 1.F 2.H 3.K 4.E 5.I 6.A 7.J 8.B 9.D 10.G 11.N 12.M 13.L 14.C

How'd ya' do?

Match the wrestler to the alias or identity he used at some point in his career:

1. Sting
2. Larry Booker
3. Horace Hogan
4. Bill Eadie
5. Kevin Nash
6. Louie Spiccoli
7. Raven
8. X-Pac
9. Big John Studd
10. Kevin Kelly
11. Road Warrior Hawk

A. Masked Superstar
B. The Cannonball Kid
C. Supershredder
D. Scotty Anthony
E. Nailz
F. Captain USA
G. Steve "Flash" Borden
H. Madonna's Boyfriend
I. Moondog Spot
J. Crusher Von Haig
K. The Predator

Answers: 1.G 2.I 3.K 4.A 5.C 6.H 7.D 8.B 9.F 10.E 11.J

30-35 correct: Boy howdy! You got yourself one helluva WIQ! We hate to say this, but maybe you ought to pay a little less attention to pro wrestling, and a little more to stuff like molecular biogenetics.

25-29 correct: That's still pretty damn good!

20-24 correct: Not bad, not bad. Respectable enough to call yourself a fan at any rate.

15-19 correct: Don't beat yourself up – it's nothing a bit of late-night studying won't cure.

10-14 correct: Okay, turn off that monster stereo and turn up the volume on the TV. It's time to start paying a little more attention to those mindless bits of trivia uttered by rambling, mind-wandering commentators.

5-9 correct: Where have YOU been? All brawn and no brains is not the answer, my friend. No soup for you.

0-4 correct: IS THERE A DOCTOR IN THE HOUSE???

Taz

Fed: ECW
Age: 32
Physical: 5'10", 248 lbs
Style(s): Brawler Technical
Highest Accolade: Heavyweight Champion

The Human Suplex Machine!

justin credible

Fed: ECW
Age: 25
Physical: 5'11", 228 lbs
Style(s): Technical/Brawler
Highest Accolade: Defeating Tommy Dreamer

New Jack

Fed: ECW

Age: 36

Physical: 5'11", 230 lbs

Style(s): Brawler

Highest Accolade: 2-Time ECW Tag Team Champion (with Mustafa)

Sabu

Fed: ECW
Age: 36
Physical: 5'11", 222 lbs
Style(s): High Flyer
Highest Accolade: ECW World
Champion

spike dudley

Little sexy, the giant killer

super nova

High-flying mayhem

Super Crazy

Fed: ECW
Age: 24
Physical: 5'9", 198 lbs
Style(s): Luchador
Highest Accolade: Two-time UWA
World Welterweight Title

High-Flyin' Madness

Steve Corino

Fed: ECW
Age: 26
Physical: 6'1", 205 lbs
Style(s): Mat Wrestler
Highest Accolade: Had a World Title Match

Talks like a Lawyer...Wrestles like One Too!

Rotten to the Core!

Axl Rotten

Fed: ECW
Age: 28
Physical: 6'2", 295 lbs
Style(s): Brawler
Highest Accolade: ECW Tag Team Champion

Chris Candido

Back for Good, or Weekend Pass?

The Dudley Boyz: Buh Buh Ray, D-Von, Sign Guy & Joel Gertner

DUDLEY BOYZ

The Revenge of the Nerds!

Lance Storm

Fed:: ECW
Age: 30
Physical: 5'11", 225 lbs
Style(s): Power Moves
Highest Accolade: ECW Tag Team
  Champion (with Chris Candido)

Shane Douglas

Fed: ECW
Age: 35
Physical: 5'11", 243 lbs
Style(s): Technical/Brawler
Highest Accolade: ECW World Champion

Rob Van Dam

Age: 28
Fed: ECW
Height: 5'10"
Weight: 232 lbs
Style: High Flyer/Hardcore
Highest Accolade: ECW TV title
Hometown: Battle Creek, Mich.

van dam

1989

Trained with The Sheik and his nephew Sabu (his current tag team partner). At the time, he'd already studied kickboxing, and had an interest in becoming a pro wrestler. The name Rob Van Dam would be given to him by Ron Slinker in the USWA.

1990

Made his debut, though only wrestled sporadically in lesser-known indies until entering the USWA in '91.

1992

Had first tour with "All Japan Pro Wrestling." He'd go in to work a lot with Baba's promotion over the next several years.

1993

Was brought in to WCW by Bill Watts and wrestled as Robbie V. However, he didn't stay long, as there was very little talent in the company at the time that wrestled in his style. Reportedly Sabu had the same problem.

1996

Paul Heyman called him out of the blue about working with ECW. He declined at first, but finally agreed in 1996, entering a program with longtime friend Sabu. He's spent the majority of his time since working with Sabu in some form or another.

1997

The biggest angle he's been involved in to date remains the "Respect Match" with Sabu. In fact, it still continues. The feud stems from Van Dam's refusal to shake Sabu's hand after the latter won a match. It led to a bitter feud for respect that spawned several excellent matches on ECW television.

1998

Teamed with Sabu to win the tag team championships from Chris Candido and Lance Storm. Defeated Bam Bam Bigelow for the TV title on April 4 in Buffalo, N.Y. He's held the title since, his first ECW singles championship. He and Sabu won the tag titles again defeating the Dudleys in the ECW arena.

1999

Van Dam remains in ECW, one of the top performers in the federation. Since he's had opportunities to go to the big feds, don't look for him to be making any moves in the near future—unless he's offered a contract that really works for him. He's also starred in several martial-arts movies, including "Blood Moon" and "Superfights"." He remains one of the most popular stars in ECW, and his battles with Sabu have been defined as classics.

Tammy Bytch
ecw

Lance is one lucky guy!

Jasmine
ecw

Hanging out at "Living Dangerously"

TAMMY LYNN

ecw

Chris,
you lucky
sonofagun!

Francine
ecw
Thinking of you.

in memoriam. . .

Owen Hart
and
Rick Rude

Owen Hart (real name: Owen Hart)

Age: 32
Fed: WWF
Weight: 226 lbs
Style: High Flyer/Technical
Highest Accolade: WWF Intercontinental Champion
Native Country: Canada

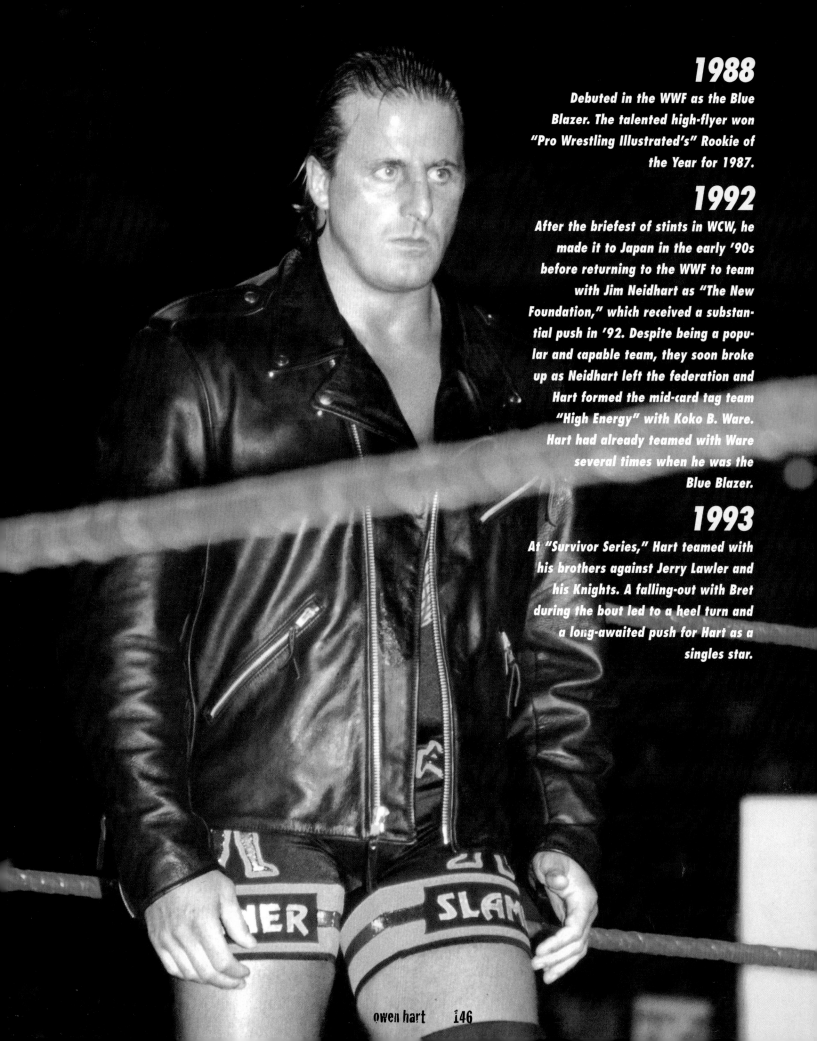

1988

Debuted in the WWF as the Blue Blazer. The talented high-flyer won "Pro Wrestling Illustrated's" Rookie of the Year for 1987.

1992

After the briefest of stints in WCW, he made it to Japan in the early '90s before returning to the WWF to team with Jim Neidhart as "The New Foundation," which received a substantial push in '92. Despite being a popular and capable team, they soon broke up as Neidhart left the federation and Hart formed the mid-card tag team "High Energy" with Koko B. Ware. Hart had already teamed with Ware several times when he was the Blue Blazer.

1993

At "Survivor Series," Hart teamed with his brothers against Jerry Lawler and his Knights. A falling-out with Bret during the bout led to a heel turn and a long-awaited push for Hart as a singles star.

1994

Defeated Bret cleanly in the opener of "Wrestlemania X" at 20:21. The match remains one of the greatest encounters in "Wrestlemania" history. That June, Neidhart returned to the federation and helped Owen Hart defeat Razor Ramon in the finals of the 2nd annual "King of the Ring" tournament, after Hart had already put away Tatanka and the 1-2-3 kid (X-Pac) in opening rounds. Hart feuded with Bret over the world title for the rest of the year as the pair put on a string of excellent matches, including a steel-cage encounter at "Summerslam" that marked the return of the "British Bulldog" Davey Boy Smith to the federation. Smith teamed with Bret against Owen and Neidhart on "Raw," and headlined cards around the U.S. and in Europe.

1995

Teamed with Yokozuna to win his first world title, the WWF tag belts, at "Wrestlemania XI." The team, managed by Jim Cornette, rolled through '95, dominating a feud against the British Bulldog and Lex Luger while holding teams such as The Smoking Gunns and Men on a Mission at bay.

1996

Bulldog, now a heel, teamed with Hart to win the tag straps. The duo was so good in the ring that it often got loud ovations, despite playing the part of "rulebreakers."

1997

Lost in the finals of the European Championship tournament in Germany to Smith shortly before "Wrestlemania." The match was a total classic. Shortly thereafter, Bret turned heel and reunited the family to form the New Hart Foundation, which included the late great Brian Pillman and a returning Neidhart. Defeated Rocky Maivia for the Intercontinental Title April 27 on "Raw." He lost it to Steve Austin at "Summerslam" in August. It's said that the scripted ending to the match involved Owen piledriving Austin multiple times; but on the first (an inverted piledriver with no neck support), Austin's neck was severly damaged, and he lost feeling in his body for several minutes. Hart, immediately aware he was injured, worked the fans while Austin recovered somewhat. Owen then set himself up to be rolled up from behind, as Austin interpreted his intent correctly and made an extremely weak cover. The finish remains one of the worst looking in history, but is acknowledged as a work of intuitiveness and quick thinking on the part of both stars. After Austin was forced to forfeit the title due to injury, Hart won an ensuing tournament to decide the new champion on Oct. 5 (the same tragic day Brian Pillman was found dead in his hotel room). He dropped the title to Austin in a short, no-bumps match at the "Survivor Series" on Nov. 9, putting Austin over cleanly with the stunner.

1998

Turned face after brother Bret was screwed at the "Survivor Series," but quickly reverted to heel after a feud with Hunter Hearst Helmsley for the Euro title, which he held for two months.

1999

Formed a successful tag team with Jeff Jarrett and won the tag team titles the day after the "Royal Rumble." Combined, the new champions had the potential to be the best since Hart teamed with Davey Boy Smith and before.

Died on May 23, 1999, at the age of 34.

Rick Rude
1958-1999

The world says farewell to a wrestling icon

By Dave Meltzer

The death of Rick Rude on April 20 marked the latest tragedy to befall professional wrestling. Rude passed away that evening of a heart attack after being rushed to the North Fulton Medical Center near his home in Alpharetta, Ga., an Atlanta suburb. He was 40.

At the time of his death, Rude had been working with World Championship Wrestling as an announcer for the "Backstage Blast" pay-per-view airings of *Nitro* on DirecTV once a month. This job came after he was removed from his role as childhood friend Curt Hennig's on-camera manager.

Rude also had been training for an in-ring comeback nearly five years after he suffered a career-threatening broken back in a May 1, 1994, match against Sting at the Fukuoka Dome. He reportedly had been trying to get out of his WCW contract since December 1998, presumably to wrestle in the World Wrestling Federation.

On April 20, Rude, whose legal name was Richard Erwin Rood, had taken his 8-year-old son to school, attended a martial arts class and gone out to hit some golf balls. At about 5 P.M., his wife returned from shopping and found him on the floor barely breathing and with a light pulse. She called 911, and he was revived briefly in an ambulance before suffering cardiac arrest in the hospital. The cause of Rude's heart attack was not immediately known.

In the wrestling community, Rude was remembered as a consummate showman and an icon in the sport.

"He was a great entertainer," said his wife Michelle, 33. "He was nothing like the person in the ring. He was a great family man. He lived for his kids, and he ate and slept wrestling."

Richard Rood was born Dec. 7, 1958, and grew up in Robbinsdale, Minn. After high school, he was working as a bouncer, and he was known for being so powerful that he often could knock people out with an open-handed slap.

Although very muscular, he had the look of being in great condition, but not necessarily possessing great power. Obviously those looks were deceiving as he had incredible grip strength and was well-known as a tough street fighter. He also was a noted arm wrestler, finishing sixth in the world championships in Las Vegas in the light heavyweight division in 1983.

"You can talk about this and that guy being a great shooter," said Eddie Sharkey, who trained Rood, Barry Darsow, The Road Warriors, Nikita Koloff and numerous other wrestlers. "But this guy kicked more ass than any of them. People didn't realize how tough this guy was. He'd slap guys with an open hand and it looked like their head exploded."

Growing up in Minneapolis in the early '80s – where wrestling was part of the local culture with the likes of Verne Gagne, Jesse Ventura and later peaking with Hulk Hogan – it was natural for gym rats and bouncers like Rood to think about a pro wrestling career. In 1981, Rood was training for a Tough Man contest and had a 2-0 record as an amateur boxer training under Papa Joe Daszciewicz. Some say he could have made a lot of money as a boxer, but Rood gravitated toward pro wrestling and made a lot more. By 1982, Rood had broken into wrestling, but he barely had enough money for gas to get to his matches and often would sleep in his car.

At the time, Ole Anderson, who was running Georgia Championship Wrestling, Inc., was starving for new talent, so he brought Rood and Darsow in. Rood was given a minor push at the beginning as a babyface with the gimmick – creatively enough – as the toughest bouncer in Minneapolis. He didn't last long in Georgia, though, and was sent to work briefly for Jim Crockett in the Carolinas as jobber Ricky Rood, and later Watts in the Mid-South territory as a good-looking undercard babyface.

But it was Jerry Jarrett who made Rood a star after he had only about one year full-time in the business. Jarrett changed his name to "Ravishing Rick Rude" and gave him the popular song "Smooth Operator" as his ring music. He also was given a monstrous heel push with valet Angel, playing the role he'd continue to play throughout his active career. Rude initially wasn't all that good in the ring, but since

most of his main events were against Jerry Lawler, there was no problem in him headlining.

His interviews weren't polished either, although the potential was there. His strong delivery and arrogant personality made people believe he hated opponents like Lawler, Austin Idol, Randy Savage and the Fabulous Ones, and fans hated him for it. Rude, with his movie-star looks and chiseled physique, had memorable programs during a period when Jarrett's business was extremely strong, working as the main heel in the company for several months. Somewhere along the way, Angel disappeared, but Rude was made as a star.

He went next to Florida, under Dory Funk as booker. Rude had a good look, but in a

territory based more on in-ring performance, he was usually paired as a tag team with Jesse Barr. Rude was put on top as Southern heavyweight champion, his most notable feud being with Wahoo McDaniel.

Rude's next stop was Texas starting in late 1985 for World Class Championship Wrestling, where he became the first-ever WCWA world heavyweight champion. In the biggest show to that point in his career, he worked the semi-main event on the May 4, 1986, show in Texas Stadium. He defended the WCWA title, winning via DQ against Bruiser Brody.

The next stop was Jim Crockett's office, which at this point had gotten the TBS contract and thus was Vince McMahon's only real national competitor during the late '80s. Rude arrived in late 1986, and immediately was programmed as a mid-card heel feuding with old rival McDaniel. Eventually he was put together as a heel tag team with Manny Fernandez, who had just turned on Dusty Rhodes, and both were managed by Paul Jones. The two spent several months feuding with the Rock & Roll Express over the NWA world tag-team titles, which Rude and Fernandez quickly won. In May of 1987, Rude, without giving notice or dropping the belts, left while holding one half of the tag-team title.

Once Rude had moved on and joined the WWF, he was not an instant success. He languished in undercards for several months until coming up with the catch-phrase entrance and hitting it big with his first program. Perhaps his most memorable of all was with Jake Roberts, which started when he tried to hit on Roberts's wife Cheryl in an angle that was apparently years ahead of its time. Even though Roberts pinned Rude every night, Rude was so arrogant that he continued to get great heat everywhere he went and got over stronger. The feud continued for most of 1988, with Rude eventually being managed by Bobby Heenan.

His other big program of his WWF era was with the Ultimate Warrior. Rude scored one of the first pinfalls on Warrior when he won the Intercontinental Title on April 2, 1989, at "Wrestlemania V," leading to Warrior regaining the belt at the second annual "SummerSlam" on August 28, 1989. By this point, Rude had upped his workrate to where he became almost a bumping machine, which made him one of the few who could get a good match out of Warrior.

Of course, this also led to numerous injuries. After Warrior had captured the WWF title from Hulk Hogan at "Wrestlemania VI," Rude, who had largely feuded with Dusty Rhodes, was elevated to the top of the cards, with the storyline being that he was the one who had beaten Warrior for the IC title, climaxing with Warrior winning a cage match in the main event at "SummerSlam" on August 27, 1990. As it turned out, this was the only PPV show that he headlined as a single.

His WWF career ended shortly after his "Summer-Slam" main event after a dispute with Vince McMahon. While Rude was out of action with a torn tricep, the WWF continued to advertise him for a house show run against Warrior. While business was disappointing during this period, as Warrior was a weaker-than-expected draw as champion after Hogan, Rude was still the heel challenging for the title in all the advertising in the top arenas. Rude felt that his name was being used to draw the houses, but McMahon was paying him very little, based on the fact he wasn't wrestling on those shows. In those days before significant guaranteed money contracts, injured wrestlers were not well paid until they got back into action. Rude eventually quit the company over not getting paid main event money on those shows.

Still, Michelle Rood said, "Vince (McMahon) always treated my husband very well. He goes by talent. Some other promoters didn't go by talent. Rick spoke what he felt. A lot of promoters didn't like that. Vince respected that and understood that. Others didn't and held it against him."

Rude worked independents and All Japan until his WWF contract expired. His style wasn't considered Japan-friendly, although he proved that wrong as he did very well with New Japan on big shows over the next two years after he signed with WCW. After his WWF deal expired, on October 27, 1991, he debuted with WCW under a mask as The Halloween Phantom, using the Rude Awakening on Tom Zenk in 1:27 and getting the mega-push. Three weeks later, he captured the U.S. title from Sting due to outside interference from Lex Luger, beginning the last memorable feud of his active career.

Rude's career peaked in 1992, when he was the best heel in the business and headlined numerous house shows against Sting. But just as he really hit his stride as an all-around performer, injuries began breaking him down. Rude feuded mainly with Steamboat over the U.S. title in early 1992 in matches that were generally considered good but not great. What may have been the best match of his career was on August 12, 1992, at the finals of both the G-1 and NWA world heavyweight title tournament, losing to Masahiro Chono at Tokyo Sumo Hall. He is the only foreigner ever to go to the finals of a G-1 tournament.

Ultimately, Rude and Sting were tearing houses down with classic U.S. title matches, with Rude being his bumping machine until he was sidelined with two bulging discs, one of which pressed on a nerve. Watts, in charge of WCW at the time, decided Rude had to vacate the title because he was going to be out of action for several weeks. Rude eventually returned, but was never the same in the ring.

By this point, though, his reputation in wrestling was strong enough that it didn't really matter. He was scheduled to win the NWA world heavyweight title from Ric Flair on Sept. 19, 1993, in Houston at the "Fall Brawl" pay-per-view. Interviews were taped that summer – with Rude holding the belt and talking about upcoming defenses – long before the Flair match was even announced. The NWA Board of Governors reportedly was upset at WCW for making the title change without consulting with the board first and voted to refuse to allow the change. This led to the final WCW/NWA split.

The final match of Rude's career as an active pro wrestler took place two weeks later. With his wife expecting the couple's second child, Marissa, they induced labor so he could be there for the birth on the morning of April 27, 1994. He had to leave later that day for Japan, where he was scheduled to win back a

world title. While wrestling Sting at the Fukuoka Dome, Sting did a running-over-the-top rope dive. Rude caught Sting, but he had a mishap on an elevated board that surrounded the ringside area and blew out his C-4 and C-5 vertebrae. Rude blamed Sting for being careless in where he dove, and there was tremendous heat between the two. Rude got up and won the title with a piledriver and a kneedrop off the top rope after distraction from valet Lady Love (who worked his corner in those days only on Japan tours).

Rude never wrestled again, and a few weeks later the title change was rescinded and given back to Sting due to the controversy surrounding the finish. Rude was injured and, in very bitter fashion, gone from WCW.

"He was 35 years old and in the second year of the biggest contract he ever signed," his wife said. "And then it basically ended. That just killed him. He was a great entertainer, and it really hurt him that he couldn't perform. Even at the risk of injuring himself seriously, he'd have tried it again."

Rude was out of wrestling for the next three years and living in Tampa. He eventually returned to ECW in 1997 as a television announcer there to screw with Shane Douglas, until turning on Tommy Dreamer. WWF also hired him to work television tapings as an "insurance policy" with Shawn Michaels and Hunter Hearst Helmsley in the original incarnation of DX, before he stunned both groups (which he was working for simultaneously without a contract) by signing with WCW.

Rude's legacy in life, of course, surpassed the one he left in pro wrestling. Rude's rough exterior camouflaged the family man who talked excitedly to other wrestlers about his three children – Little Rick, 8; Marissa, 5; and Colton, 21 months. And friends noted in his passing that, outside the ring, he was the one person you'd want to have most as backup in a tough situation. Why? Because you wouldn't have to worry if he'd be there for you.

A Wrestling
Dictionary of Terms

Angle - (n) The storyline of a wrestling match or feud. **Face** - (n) The good guy. **Gimmick** - (n) Any prop or persona used in wrestling. Mortis' Skull on a Stick (Yorick) or the Goddwins' Slop Bucket are gimmicks, while their personae are also gimmicks. (v) To change or rig something. "They gimmicked the ring mat so the Undertaker could break through it to grab Diesel." **Heat** - (n) The crowd response, or the response from other people in the business. The entire purpose of a face or heel is to generate heat from the crowd. Heat is not necessarily always meant negatively. Sting or Shamrock can get a lot of heat, even though they are faces. "Shawn Michaels got a lot of heat from other people in the WWF because of his arrogant attitude." **Heel** - (n) The bad guy, and I don't mean Razor Ramon. **Job** - (v) To lose the match. "At 'Starrcade,' we saw Hulk Hogan job to Sting." (n) The loss of a match. "Before the match, the booker told the new guy he was going to do the job tonight." **Jobber** - (n) A person who typically loses their matches and doesn't have a gimmick. These are the nameless people who are beaten up each week. They are roughly the equivalent of the no-name guys in the red shirts who would beam down to the planet with Captain Kirk on *Star Trek* only to die a quick and horrible death.

Kayfabe - (n) The reason why wrestlers will not admit that anything is staged. Kayfabe is the code of silence practiced in the business to keep the trade secrets within the business. **Mark** - (n) A person who believes everything in wrestling is real. Also a term used by wrestlers to refer to any fan or anyone watching. There are several degrees of marks. Whether you like it or not, we are all marks—otherwise, we wouldn't be watching. It is possible to be a mark for only certain feds or wrestlers: "nWo mark" or "Shawn Michaels mark." (v) To lose control during a wrestling event. "Did you see that guy completely mark out when Kevin Nash came into the bar? It was embarrassing." **Over** - (adj) To be popular with the crowd. "I can't believe how over Steve Austin has been since 'Wrestlemania.'" Another term you will hear is "put over." This commonly refers to a star or veteran who loses to a new talent or takes them under their wing to help the newcomer establish their career. "Chris Benoit really wasn't big in the business until Kevin Sullivan put him over." **Shoot** - (n) An event that is not planned or is a surprise to the participants involved. Despite popular belief, shoots do happen. They are not always in matches, but most often they are in the form of interviews on live television where wrestlers will say things they are not supposed to in order to put pressure on people in the business. (v) The act of committing a shoot. "I couldn't believe it when Brian Pillman decided to shoot on Kevin Sullivan by leaving the match."

Smart - (n) Any person who understands the business behind professional wrestling. The majority of people who think they are smarts are not. As a matter of fact, when someone comes out and says they are a smart, there is a very good chance they are not. Knowing that there is an element of entertainment to it all is not enough. Being able to understand the logic behind the business decisions in the business is a big part of it. You don't decide if you are a smart—other people do. **Turn** - (n) To change from heel status to face status or vice versa. **Tweener** - (n) A wrestler who doesn't fit into the traditional heel or face role. This is becoming more and more common these days. A good example of a tweener is Kevin Nash (and to a lesser degree, Scott Hall) of the nWo. While these men have committed heel acts, they still are very popular with the fans and often get a face reaction from the crowd. **Work** - (n) A staged incident or act. "People are saying that Woman and Chris Benoit are having an affair, but I bet that it is a work."